Soft Toys

Previously published as part of

'The Big Book of Soft Toys'

Soft Toys

Previously published as part of
'The Big Book of Soft Toys'

MABS TYLER

photographs by Gina Harris

line illustrations by John Kingsford

PAN BOOKS LONDON and SYDNEY

First published 1972 as part of *The Big Book of Soft Toys*
by Wolfe Publishing Ltd
This edition published 1974 by Pan Books Ltd,
Cavaye Place, London SW10 9PG
2nd printing 1976
© Mabs Tyler and Wolfe Publishing Ltd 1972
ISBN 0 330 23865 5

Printed by Cripplegate Printing Co Ltd
Edenbridge, Kent

TO ANGELA

Contents

Introduction

Since Before recorded memory the making of toys has been among the most satisfying of domestic accomplishments.

The most popular of all toys, from then until now, has been the one which was right for the child for whom it was designed.

Soft Toys offers a range of toys which, while not demanding a skill beyond that of the average aunt, mother or grandmother, contains something which will please most children.

Many of the toys, in fact, are simple enough in design for quite young children to make for themselves. And these simple shapes can be turned into something more decorative and elaborate by colourful embroidery.

Before starting to make any of the toys it is important to read the General Hints given below.

Acknowledgements
Many thanks must be given to friends and students for practical help with drawings, sewing and checking, and to all who gave encouragement and showed interest in the book's progress.

General Hints

READ ALL INSTRUCTIONS FULLY BEFORE STARTING TO MAKE A TOY

Patterns when cut out in thin card (templates) are easier to trace round, and they last longer.

Mark on each template (a) the number of pieces to be cut from it, (b) any directions for sewing.

Keep all the templates for each toy fastened together. Place the biggest templates on the fabric first.

Cut out all the necessary pieces for the toy before starting to sew it.

Keep all the pieces for the toy together in a bag.

Embroider only simple designs on any small parts.

When sewing the parts together check that all decorated sides will be on the outside of the toy, e.g. balls, dice.

Be careful to pair right and left sides, especially when embroidering, e.g. animal sides, wings.

Leave openings for stuffing in the least noticeable places.

Use stuffing in small, soft pieces to make a smooth toy.

Do not overfill slither toys, or they may be too heavy to play with easily.

Have no hanging pieces, loose decoration or long embroidery stitches on toys designed to be much handled.

When sewing stockinette or other similar 'stretchy' fabric, use a longer stitch, preferably a back stitch, to give elasticity.

Tack fur and fur fabric and long-piled fabric on the wrong side with small stitches, leaving the stitches in for added strength.

Grid System
The pattern for each toy is overlaid by a blue grid. Each square on this grid represents 2.5 cm (1"). To transfer the pattern, draw a grid of 2.5 cm (1") squares. On this grid mark with dots where the lines of the drawing cross the lines of the blue grid.

There are two sizes of grid used in this book. The very small squares will have to be multiplied by 4, and the larger squares multiplied by 2 to bring them up to 2.5 cm (1"). You can, of course, make the toys larger than their intended size by drawing out your own grid of, say, 5 cm (2") squares.

Using felt
No allowance need be made for turnings because felt does not fray.

There is no 'right' or 'wrong' side.

Use a very sharply pointed pencil for tracing; never use ball-point pens or felt-tip pens.

Place pattern and fabric on a hard surface to give a clearer outline.

Use a white pencil or tailor's chalk on dark colours.

Keep the traced side as the wrong side when sewing the toy.

When cutting two matching pieces from a template, e.g. two sides of an animal, reverse the template or pattern when tracing the second piece so that the pencil marks on both pieces will be on the inside of the finished toy.

Cut inside the pencil lines to avoid grubby seams.

Always pin and tack close to the edge to avoid dirty marks.

When leaving work unfinished, stick needle under finished embroidery, or on the edge.

Mark the positions of features, etc, with tacking threads, *not* pencil.

To transfer a design for embroidering, trace the design on to thin paper, place it in position on the felt and work small running stitches in a contrasting colour through both paper and felt, afterwards tearing away the paper. The running stitches can be pulled out when the embroidery is finished.

Do not pull embroidery stitches too tight or the felt will pucker.

Sewing can be done on the right side.

Using fabric

Trace round the template on to the wrong side of the fabric and cut 1.25 cm ($\frac{1}{2}$") outside the line to allow for turnings.

When cutting two matching pieces from a template, e.g. two sides of an animal, reverse the template for the second piece so that the wrong side of the material will be on the inside of the toy.

Sew or stitch on the pencil line.

After sewing trim off the surplus seam allowance.

Snip 'v's out of all curves.

Snip into all corners as close to the stitching as possible to keep seams flat.

Use fabric with a firm, close weave. Loosely woven fabric, unless it is lined, will not keep in the stuffing.

Tack the pieces together outside the stitching line.

Practise sewing doll's features on paper or fabric cut to the same size as the doll's face before drawing or embroidering on to the toy.

Useful things to have

Sharp cutting-out scissors.

Scissors for cutting paper and card.

Small, very sharply pointed scissors.

A selection of needles.

Wire nippers.

Stuffing sticks — a blunted pencil, blunted wooden skewer, blunted orange stick, blunted cocktail stick.

Very sharp pencils, black and white, or white tailor's chalk.

Felt-tip pens — black, red, brown, blue.

Transparent thread.

Tape measure.

Ruler.

A pair of compasses.

Masking tape.

Colourless upholstery adhesive.

Thin card.

Tracing paper.

Piece box containing remnants and scraps of various fabrics, lace, fur, fur fabric, old nylon stockings, suede or kid gloves, Christmas ribbons and cords, sequins, beads, foam rubber, pipe cleaners.

Terms

Gingham — closely woven, thin cotton material, generally in a variety of checked and striped patterns.

Courtelle — fluffy-pile, man-made jersey fabric, used for dressing gowns.

Vilene — man-made compressed fibre, used for interlining; in various thicknesses, does not fray.

Fusible Vilene can be ironed on to fabrics as a backing, so preventing any fraying.

Wadding — compressed cotton fibres, enclosed in a very thin skin to make a flat padding.

Tarlatan — stiffened, loosely woven cotton material, used to make stiff ballet tutus.

Calico — firmly woven, strong cotton material, white or unbleached (sheeting).

Crash — coarsely woven, unbleached linen, very strong.

Cambric — finely woven, soft cotton material, used for handkerchiefs.

Poplin — firmly woven cotton material with smooth, semi-shiny surface.

Kapok — fluffy, loose fibres, used for stuffing.

Ricrac braid — decorative braid in which threads are pulled tighter on one side, giving it a wavy line.

Velcro — a type of fastener comprising two pieces, one with hooks and the other with loops, which hold firmly when pressed together.

Masking tape — an adhesive, strong paper tape.

Dowel rod — thin, hard, round wooden rod.

Felt-tip pens — marker pens with an ink reservoir, thin fibre tips for fine work and thick felt tips for broader outlines.

Pipe cleaner chenille — a continuous length (up to ten feet) of thin, pliable wire encased in a fluffy, thick covering.

Dolly pegs — old-fashioned wooden clothes pegs cut in one piece, with a round knob and two legs.

Lurex thread — a fine metal thread in gold, silver and colours.

Stitches

Running stitch

can be used for seaming together two pieces of thin or medium thicknesses of fabric or, with added variations, as a decorative stitch. Work from left to right, putting the needle in and out in one motion and keeping the spaces the same size as the stitches.

Variations on running stitch

Whipped. Thread through each running stitch in the same direction to give a corded effect.

Double whipped. Work two rows of threading, the second one in the opposite direction from the first one.

Threaded. Thread up through one stitch and down through the next one.

Double threaded. Two rows of threading are worked, the second one in the opposite direction to the first.

Block running. Rows of running stitches are worked with stitches exactly above each other. These can be threaded and double threaded, whipped and double whipped. A check design is obtained if rows of three stitches are worked with the second rows of blocks in the spaces underneath the first row and so on.

BACK STITCH

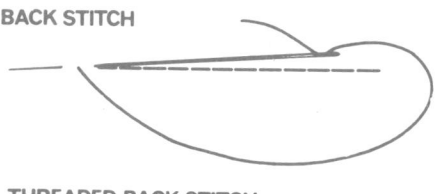

THREADED BACK STITCH

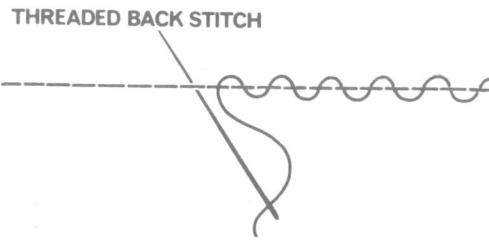

Back stitch. Work one running stitch. Insert the needle into the same hole, bringing it out a stitch's length to the left. Continue, working back into each previous stitch, completely filling the space. Back stitch can be threaded and double threaded, whipped and double whipped.

Chain stitch. Bring the thread out on the right side of the work and hold it under the left thumb. Put the needle back into the same hole, bringing it out again over the held thread. Do not pull the thread too tight. This stitch can be whipped and threaded.

DOUBLE RUNNING

Double running. Work a second row of running stitches on top of the first row so that the second row of stitches fill in the spaces in between the stitches of the first row. This can be used as an alternative to back stitch.

CHAIN

WHIPPED CHAIN — can also be threaded

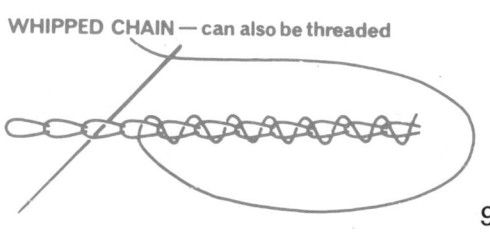

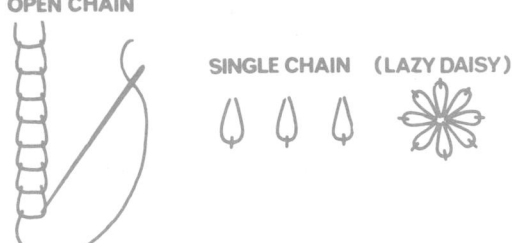

SINGLE CHAIN (LAZY DAISY)

Open chain stitch. This is formed in the same way as chain stitch, but the needle is inserted to the right of the first stitch and slanted to the left, to come out under the first stitch. Keep the loop loose enough to take the second stitch.

Fly stitch. This too is a form of open chain stitch. Hold the thread under the left thumb and insert the needle to the right of the first stitch, bringing it out lower down in the middle of the two stitches and over the loop. Insert the needle under the loop to hold it, bringing it out to the left under the first stitch. This stitch can be done horizontally, vertically and singly as a filling stitch.

Snail trail or coral stitch. Hold thread horizontally under left thumb. Take a slanting stitch to the left through the material and including the held thread. Gently pull up to form a knot, and repeat the process.

Buttonhole stitch. Work from left to right. Hold the thread to the right under the left thumb. Insert the needle about 3mm ($\frac{1}{8}$") above the hole, bringing it out close to the hole and over the held thread. Pull the thread to hold the loop and hold it under the thumb again. Insert the needle in line and to the right of the last stitch, bringing it out under the insertion point in line with the first stitch and over the held thread. The stitches should be at right angles to the row of loops.

Pointed buttonhole. As for buttonhole, but three buttonhole stitches are made into each hole; in the first one the needle slants down to the left, the second stitch is vertical and in the third the needle slants down to the right.

Stem stitch. Work from left to right. It is similar to back stitch in reverse, the needle brought out halfway along the last stitch and touching it, giving a corded effect.

Couching. A cord or several threads are held in position by working vertical stitches over them, close to each side of the threads.

Herring bone. Worked on two parallel lines from left to right. Bring the thread out on the top line. Take a stitch from right to left on the bottom line so that the thread slopes down to the right. Take the next stitch in the top line so that the thread slopes up to the right, crossing the previous thread.

Cross stitch. Worked on two lines. Work a row of stitches sloping from left to right between the two lines. A second row worked in the opposite direction using the same holes crosses over the first row of threads.

Joining stitches

Oversewing. Work from right to left. Hold the two edges of the material together and insert the needle at right angles from back to front through both thicknesses. Continue so, keeping the spaces even, so that the stitches will slant evenly.

Crossed oversewing is obtained by working a second row from left to right, using the same holes.

Double-locking oversewing. Work as for oversewing, but taking two stitches into each hole, so that the slanting stitch and the straight stitch from the same hole give a zigzag effect.

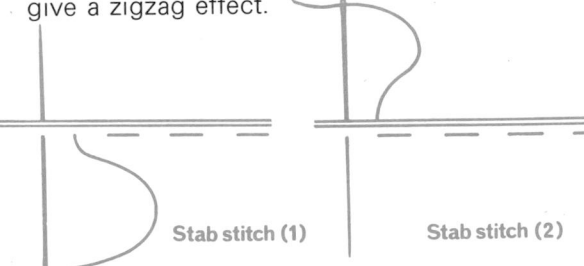

Stab stitch (1)   Stab stitch (2)

Stab stitch. This is used when joining two thick fabrics such as felt, so that one piece is not stretched more than the other, as it would be if running stitch were used. The effect is like running stitch. Insert the needle at right angles to the edges of material from front to back and then from back to front.

Fishbone stitch. This stitch makes a flat seam, not ridged as in oversewing. Place the two pieces of material with the edges butting on each other and touching. Work from right to left and take a stitch from back to front first in one piece and then in the other.

Ladder stitch. This is another flat seam join. Lay the two pieces of material with edges butting against each other. Take a small stitch parallel to the edges first in one piece and then in the other. Pull the thread firmly but not tight enough to pucker the material.

Laced buttonhole. Work buttonhole stitch on the edges of both pieces of material. Lay the two buttonholed edges butting on each other. Lace the edges together by sewing through the loops on each edge.

CHAPTER ONE

Soft toy balls

The soft balls dealt with here are made from two basic shapes, but there are many other possibilities, giving great scope for experiment and invention. All sizes of ball can be made from each of the shapes, according to the size of template used; the basic oval segment can be short and fat, or long and thin; the shape of the segment adapted by moving the position of the widest part from the centre and closer to one end of it, as in Humpty Dumpty. Other soft balls can be very attractive made from wool, wound round card rings and tied and cut for a fluffy ball, or knitted or crocheted and then filled with stuffing.

An embroidered ball in six segments

You will need:

A piece of felt measuring approximately 18 cm by 38 cm (7" by 14"); some embroidery silks for a decorated ball as in the picture; matching cotton for joining the pieces; a small piece of thin card to make a template; kapok or similar for stuffing.

Make the template

On the thin card make a cross (Fig 1) by drawing a line 15.2 cm (6") long with a second line 5 cm (2") long at right angles across the centre of it. Draw curved lines from one end of the long line to the other, touching each end of the short line to give the shape of the template from which each segment is cut (Fig 2, overleaf).

Cut out your felt

Trace round the template on the felt with a very sharp pencil six times and cut the pieces (Fig 3), keeping the traced sides as the wrong side so that any pencil marks will not show. Any embroidery to be done on the sections should be done on the separate pieces before joining them together (Fig 4). Choose fairly simple designs. Keep the stitches firm but not too tight, or the felt may pucker.

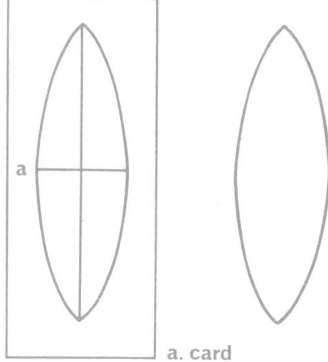

a. card

Fig 1

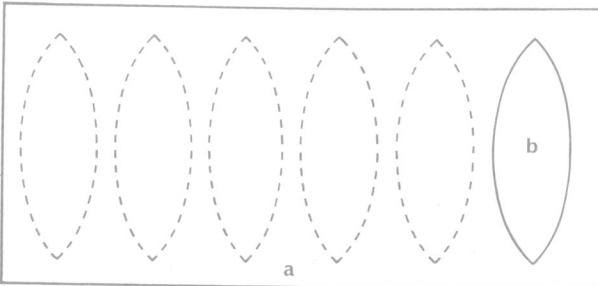

a. felt   b. template

Fig 3

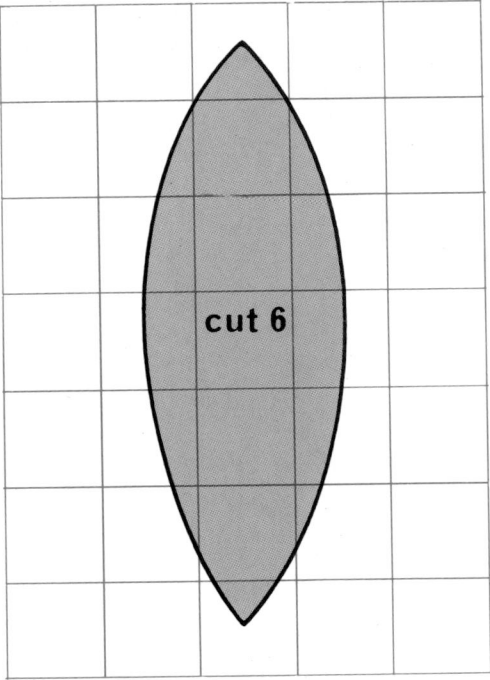

cut 6

Fig 2

Fig 4

Make up
Pin two pieces together with the right sides outside, pinning close to the edges to avoid pin marks showing, and oversew the two edges with matching cotton (Fig 5). Join the other pieces on in the same way, leaving the last two sides open. Fill it with small pieces of kapok or chosen stuffing until it is firm and smooth, and then sew up the opening.

A ball with embroidered edges
A variation on this embroidered ball can be made by embroidering the edges of each segment with blanket or buttonhole stitch and then joining the sections by lacing together the embroidery (doing this firmly so that no big spaces are left, or the stuffing will be pushed out).

A ball in four segments
Smaller balls can be made from four segments. They are, in fact, stronger because more segments mean more seams and this necessarily weakens the ball. On the other hand, larger balls are a better shape if more segments are used.

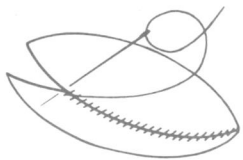

Fig 5

Find out the size
To determine the size of segments (Fig. 6): for an 8 cm (3″) ball in four segments, multiply the length by two to get an approximate circumference and divide by the number of segments,

e.g.: $8 \times 2 \div 4 = 4$ cm

$(3 \times 2 \div 4 = 1\frac{1}{2}″)$

so each segment will measure 8 cm (3″) by 4 cm (1½″).

Or for a larger playball measuring 30 cm (12″) in eight segments,

$30 \times 2 \div 8 = 7.5$ cm

$(12 \times 2 \div 8 = 3″)$

so each segment will measure 30 cm by 7.5 cm (12″ by 3″). The curves on each side of the template must be smooth and each side must match.

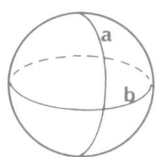

a. 8 cm (3″)
b. circumference 8 cm (3″)

Fig 6

A bouncing ball on elastic

A 10 cm (4″) or 13 cm (5″) ball would be large enough for this kind of ball. If it is bigger it will be too heavy to play with easily, or the elastic will snap.

You will need:

Felt for a light ball; or plastic material; or imitation leather; or fluffy man-made fibre; or cotton material such as gingham; kapok, and a length of round elastic.

If you are using man-made fibre or cotton, it must be sewn on the wrong side and the balls turned out before they are filled with stuffing. Cotton or fraying materials must have turnings allowed for, so after tracing the shape on the wrong side of the material, cut the pieces outside the pencil line (Fig 7), and stitch, either machine or firm back stitch (Fig 8), on the pencil line.

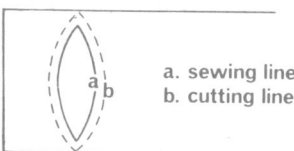

a. sewing line
b. cutting line

Fig 7

back stitch

Fig 8

Sew the knotted end of a length of elastic very firmly inside the ball before completing the stuffing and sewing up. If the joins of the pointed ends of the segments are not strong enough, cut a circle or flower motif and sew on at each end, threading the elastic through it at one end (Fig 9).

Fig 9

A giant playball

Although more sewing is involved, the actual making and handling is easy, because of its size. The one in the picture (*see* p 21) is not really a 'giant', but is 30 cm (12″) long, so that each segment measures 30 cm by 8 cm (12″ by 3″) in the middle at its widest part, tapering to a point at each end. A rainbow ball can be made by using a different colour of felt or material for each section.

Join the sections together with firm oversewing, leaving open half of the last seam. Fill quite firmly with stuffing and sew up the opening. Again a neat finish is obtained by sewing a circle over the joins of the pointed ends.

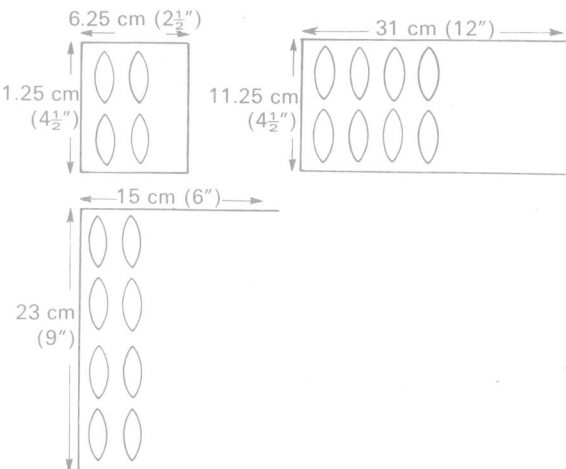

6.25 cm (2½")
11.25 cm (4½")
31 cm (12")
11.25 cm (4½")
15 cm (6")
23 cm (9")

Fig 10

Small balls for counting

You will need:

Small pieces of felt; stuffing; matching cotton; a length of fine cord; a strip of balsa wood; and five small cup hooks.

Any number of balls can be made, and in any colours, but it will probably be helpful to the young 'counter' if one colour is used for each group of balls.

The amount of felt needed will vary according to the number of balls involved. For one ball a piece 11.25 cm by 6.25 cm (4½" by 2½") will make a 5 cm (2") ball in four segments. The size will increase

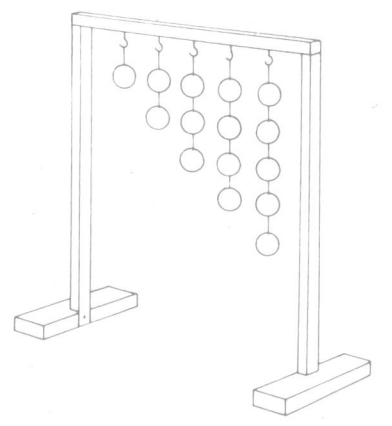

Fig 11

for each group, the final one of five balls (20 segments) needing to be 11.25 cm by 31 cm (4½" by 12") or 23 cm by 15 cm (9" by 6") (Fig 10). The pictured ones are in five distinctive colours of 5 cm (2") balls strung from hooks in a balsa wood strip. They could also be strung from a frame on a base so that they would stand up (Fig 11).

Making up

To avoid losing any of the small segments, cut only enough at one time to complete the balls for each group. Join the pieces on the right sides with oversewing, leaving the last sides open.

Make a large knot at the end of a length of fine cord — silver cord of the kind used for tying Christmas parcels was used here — and wrap a ball of kapok round the knot. Push some kapok into the felt ball and on top of that place the ball of stuffing containing the knot, with the end of cord through the opening at the pointed end of the segments (Fig 12). Push in more filling to make it firm, and sew up the opening. Make a loop in the end of the cord (Fig 13). This is number one.

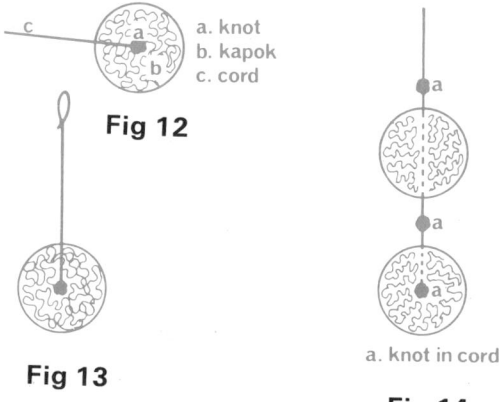

a. knot
b. kapok
c. cord

Fig 12

Fig 13

a. knot in cord

Fig 14

For number two have a slightly longer piece of cord and make the first ball on it as just described. Join up the pieces for the second ball, leaving the last two sides open. Make a knot in the cord, close to the first ball and large enough to keep the balls apart (Fig 14). Put a little filling in the ball, lay the cord in the ball so that the knot is close to the outside edge. Cover the cord closely with more filling to make a firm ball, and sew up the opening.

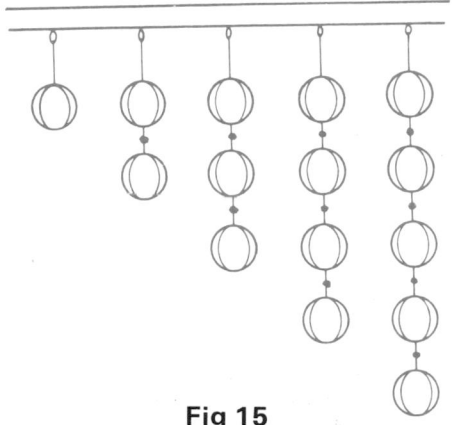

Fig 15

Fig 16

Make a template

To make a template for an 8 cm (3") ball, draw a line 8 cm (3") long and across the centre of it, at right angles, draw a line 3.75 cm (1½") long. From each end of the long line draw a curve touching each end of the short line, and cut out this segment shape in thin card.

Work on the felt

Trace round the template on the felt and cut out four shapes for each ball.

Embroider the pieces before joining them together. Join them on the right side with matching cotton, leaving the last two sides open.

Ease the kapok in smoothly in small pieces, pressing it gently into the seams to make a good round shape. Sew up the opening.

Finish off

Cut two small circles or flower shapes (Fig 16), punch a hole in the centre of them and sew at each side over the joined points. Complete the rest of the balls in the same way.

Thread round elastic into a bodkin and thread each ball through the punched holes in the ends.

Smaller felt balls

Similar small balls of 5 cm (2") length will need a larger number to stretch across the pram. Templates for these would measure 2.5 cm (1") across the middle.

Make up the rest of the groups in the same way. Tie loops in the ends of the cords so that the top balls in each section are level when hanging.

Cut a length from a piece of balsa wood, or dowel rod, screw in small cup or curtain hooks and fasten the cords to them (Fig 15).

Small balls for a baby's pram

Brightly coloured, soft felt balls are a quick and easy present to make for stringing along the front of a baby's pram.

You will need:

Pieces of felt in five or six bright colours; kapok for stuffing; matching cotton; a template of the shape of each segment.

Each ball has four segments in it; these can be all the same colour or each segment a different colour for little rainbow balls.

A ball from twelve pentagon-shaped pieces

You will need:

Felt in one colour, or two colours or many colours; stuffing; embroidery silks; a piece of thin card for a template; a design for embroidery; a protractor or a ruler with angles marked on it.

The ball can have an embroidered motif in the centre of each pentagon, or can be embroidered round all the edges which are laced together firmly and then stuffed.

Make the template

The half-size template for the ball is given here (Fig 17), but making a different-sized one is quite simple. Take the protractor or ruler. Draw a line 5 cm (2") long on the card. Place the 90° line on the protractor at the left-side end of the line and mark with a dot the 72° angle on the left (Fig 18). Join the left-side end of the line to the dot and make this second line 5 cm (2") long. Repeat this, always working from the left side of the line, to the left, making each new line 5 cm (2") long and you will eventually have your pentagon shape. Trace round the pentagon on to the felt (Fig 19) and cut out twelve shapes.

Embroidery

Always use a very finely pointed pencil for drawing on felt. Do the embroidery now before joining the sections. Designs should be simple because the shapes are quite small (Fig 20). Do not use a pencil to mark the design but draw it on thin paper, pin it on to the felt and sew the design on to the felt through the paper with small running stitches (Fig 21). Tear away the paper. The embroidery will cover most of the stitches, or they can be pulled out later.

Make up the ball in two halves. Oversew five of the pieces (Fig 22) to the sixth, one on each edge making a flower shape, and sewing on the right side. Sew the edges of the five pieces to each other, making a bowl shape (Fig 23). Repeat this with the other six pieces. The two bowl shapes are sewn together to make the ball, the points of one fitting into the 'v's on the other. Oversew them together, leaving the last two sides open. Push in the stuffing gently, easing it into the seams for a good shape. When the ball is firm, sew up the opening.

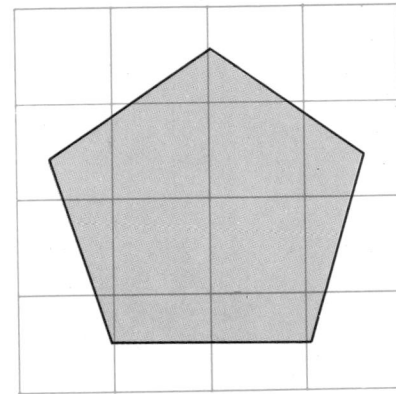

Fig 17

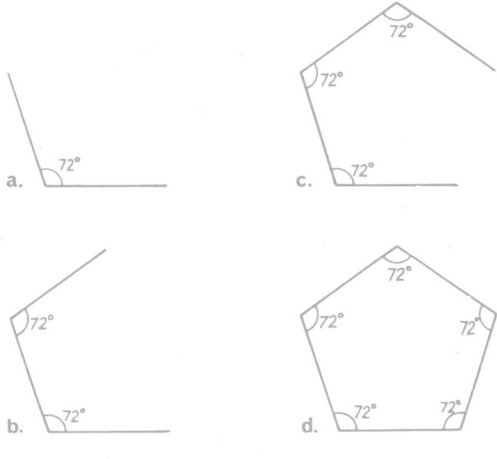

Fig 18

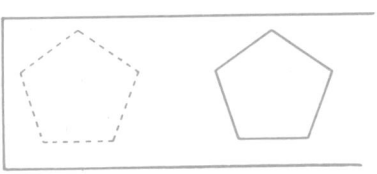

Fig 19

Fig 20

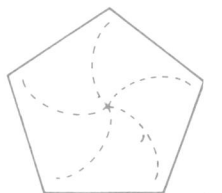

Fig 21

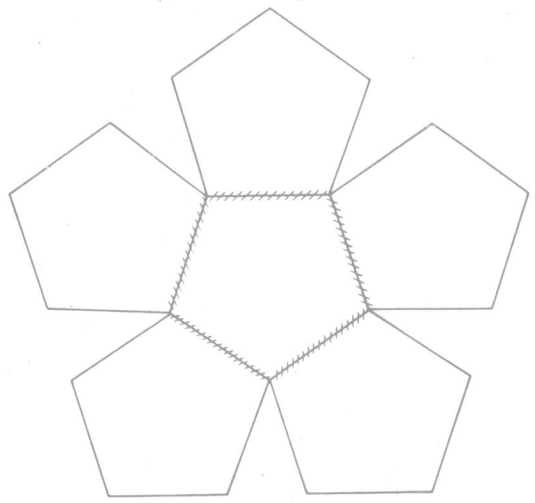

Fig 23

Fig 22

A cat-faced ball

You will need:

The same materials as for the 15 cm (6")
ball; plus two pointed ear shapes;
some scraps of green felt for eyes
and some bright green embroidery
silk.

Making up

Make up the ball following the directions
for the six-segment ball. Cut four ovals
pointed at each end, in green felt (Fig 24a)
and sew two of them on each side of the
ball, slanting in towards the centre, with
a thick black vertical line embroidered
across the centres (Fig 25). Sew straight
lines for whiskers on each side of the
centre of the face, underneath the eyes.
Sew an ear (Fig 24b) very firmly over the
eyes on each side of the ball.

The cat-faced ball can also be mounted
on a piece of dowel rod. Pad the top of the
dowel with a wad of stuffing (Fig 27) (if
necessary tie it round and round with
cotton or string) and insert it into the ball
before filling it, so that the pointed ends
of the join fit around it. Pad it securely
with more stuffing to keep it in place.

Make a rattle

Any of the balls, except the very small
ones, can be made into rattles by putting a
few dried peas or tiny stones into a small
tin box (Fig 26), wrapping the box firmly
in a ball of stuffing and inserting it in the
middle of the ball with more stuffing
wedged round it.

A rugby-shaped ball

You will need:

A piece of felt 26 cm by 33 cm (10½" by
13"); some stuffing and matching
cotton.

The template

The card template for this is long and thin,
measuring 25 cm (10") by 5 cm (2") in
the middle at the widest part, so that the
finished ball will be 30 cm (12") all round
the middle (Fig 28). Cut out six pieces
by tracing round the template and make
it up from the directions for the 15 cm (6")
ball.

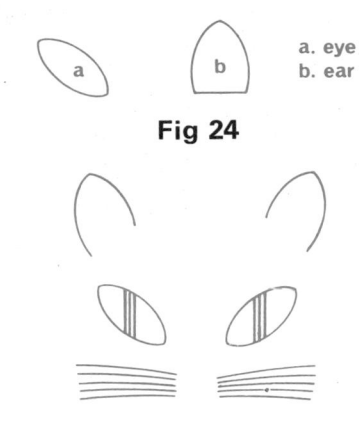

a. eye
b. ear

Fig 24

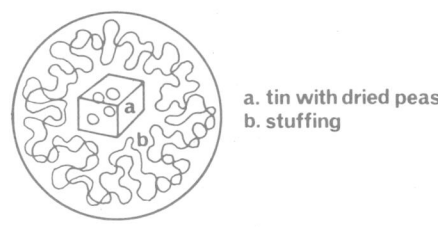

Fig 25

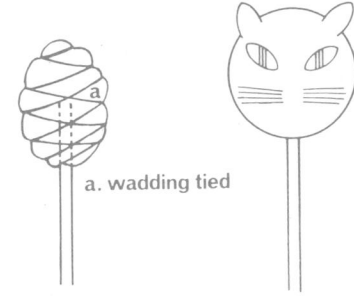

a. tin with dried peas
b. stuffing

Fig 26

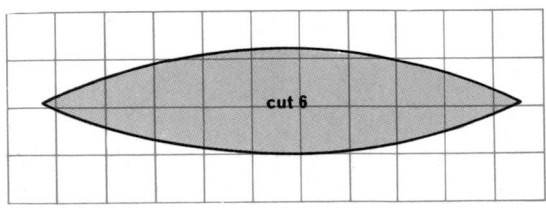

a. wadding tied

Fig 27

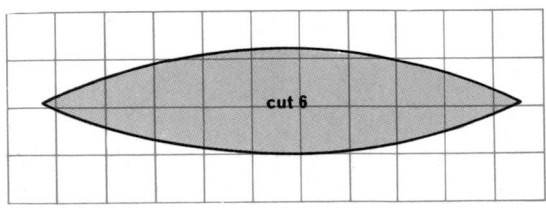

cut 6

Fig 28

Humpty Dumpty

The template for him is based on that for the 15 cm (6") ball but the cross line giving the width is placed three-quarters of the way down instead of across the middle, making the fattest part in the lower half of the shape (Fig 32).

Embroider

Make it up as for the 15 cm (6") ball. If it is to be used as a ball, then embroider features and hair and any additions of clothing to keep the ball outline smooth with no free loose pieces to hinder throwing and catching it.

For a toy

If it is to be played with as a toy, then limbs and clothes can be added like any other doll.

Cut rectangles of felt for arms and legs, joining them down the long sides and one short end. Use only a little stuffing so that the limbs are flexible, or bind together pipe cleaners to match the lengths of felt and sew the felt round them (Fig 29). Attach them at shoulders and hips, and they can then be bent to the required shape.

A sleeveless jacket of the same colour as the felt arms can be sewn on to him (Fig 30).

Cut a round white collar with a big black bow to finish it off.

Four little shoe shapes (Fig 31) in black felt can be sewn together in pairs, lightly stuffed and sewn on to the ends of the legs.

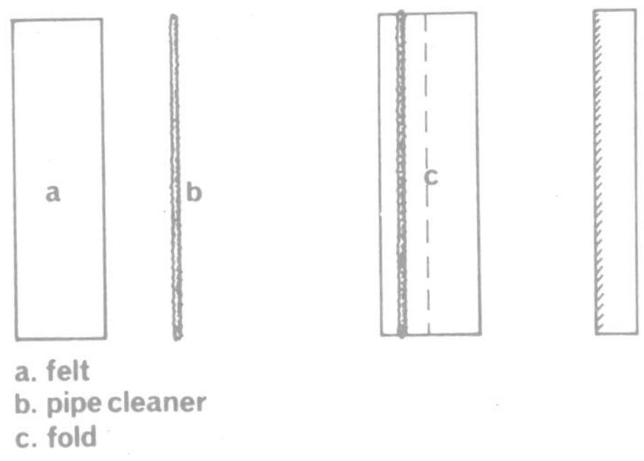

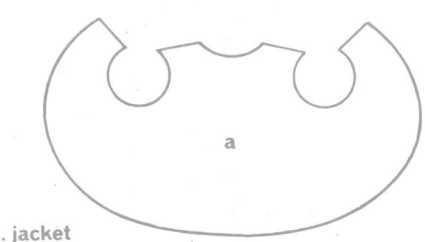

a. felt
b. pipe cleaner
c. fold

Fig 29

Fig 30

a. jacket

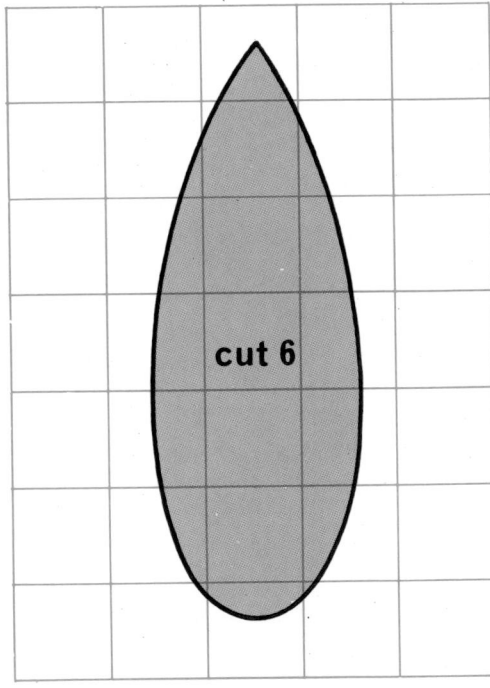

cut 6

Fig 32

 **Fig 31**

CHAPTER TWO

Dice, bricks and tiles

Many games have been invented for using dice. They are popular with young children as an aid for learning to count, for sorting, or for recognizing numbers and groups of objects. Big, soft dice are easy to handle in play and, made in bright colours, are attractive too. Felt is easy to work with because it does not fray, but other fabrics can be used successfully provided that turnings are allowed for when cutting out the shapes. Sizes shown here are 8 cm (3") and 10 cm (4") but they can of course be made to any desired size by altering the measurements of the squares. Very small dice are difficult to embroider.

Traditional dice

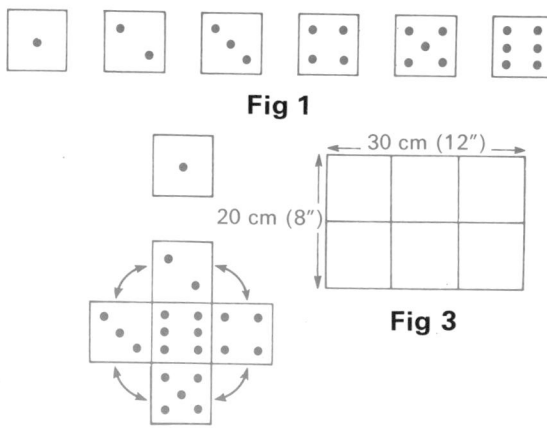

Fig 1

Fig 2

Fig 3

You will need:
Kapok or similar stuffing;
embroidery silks; matching cotton;
felt or fabric in the main colour for
the dice itself and a contrasting
colour or colours for the spots.

This one is in dark blue felt with yellow spots and is an 8 cm (3") cube.
Cut six 8 cm (3") squares from the blue felt and 21 spots from the contrasting piece. (Draw round a 2p piece.) Dice are designed in a traditional pattern and numbers must always be in the same sequence so that 1 is opposite to 6, 2 opposite to 5, and 3 opposite to 4. Sew the spots on to their squares in a traditional pattern as shown in Fig 1.
Now lay the squares in their right order. Sew one side of squares 2, 3, 4, 5 to square 6, forming a cross. Make it into a box shape by sewing up the sides (Fig 2), making sure that all the spots are on the outside. Sew two sides of remaining square 1 to the open end of the box.
Push the stuffing gently but firmly into corners and seams to keep it a good shape. Sew up the remaining two sides.

A picture cube

This soft cube with a different little picture on each side is very simple to make, and the colours you choose for the actual cube and the pictures appliquéd on it turn it into a very gay toy for a small child.

You will need:
A piece of felt 20 cm by 30 cm (8" by 12"); some small pieces of felt in bright colours; some thin card to make templates; and stuffing and embroidery silks.

Embroidered pictures

Cut the large piece of felt into six squares measuring 10 cm (4") (Fig 3). Each square must be embroidered before any sewing up is done. The six pictures in the drawing are a teapot, some balloons, a

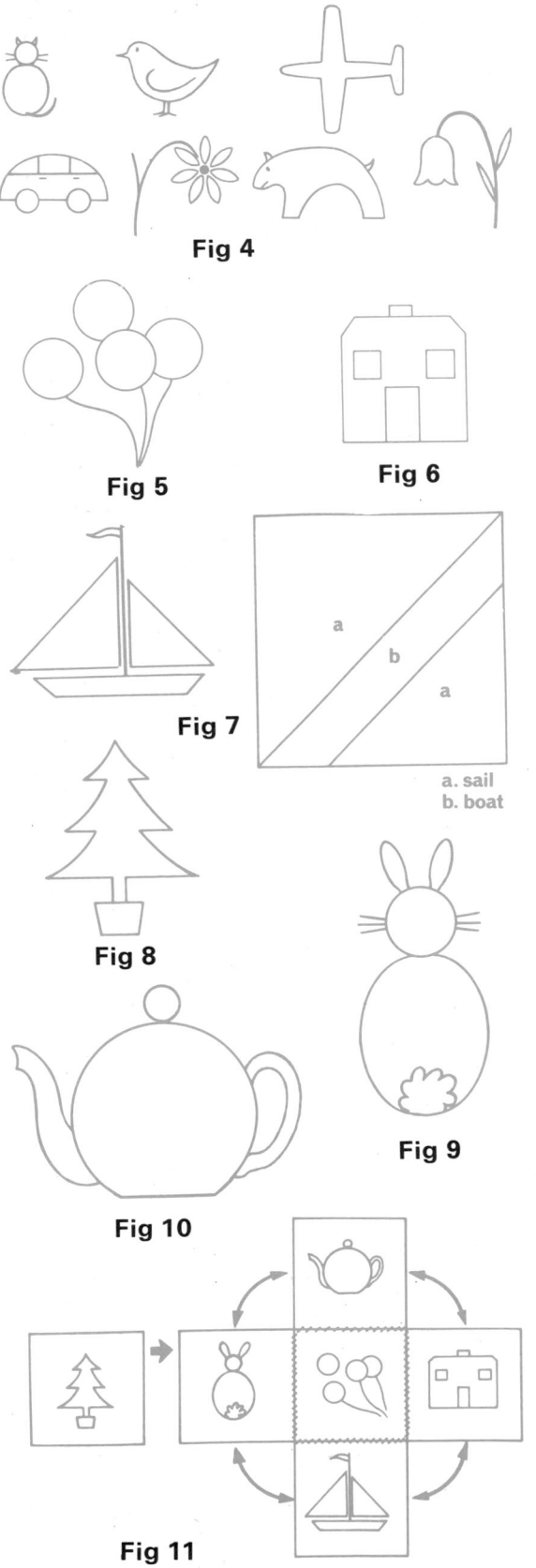

Christmas tree, a sailing ship, a rabbit and a house. Any silhouette which is not too fussy can be used: a cat, dog, bird, flower, aeroplane or car (Fig 4). The pictures are easy to trace on to the felt if they are cut out in thin card.

Balloons

The balloons are four circles traced round a 10p piece, sewn on to the square with very small stitches and their strings embroidered in running stitch (Fig 5).

A house

This is a square of purple felt with the top corners snipped off to make the roof, and a small square on top for a chimney. An oblong of green for the door and two yellow windows complete it, the whole sewn on to the square with matching cotton (Fig 6).

A sailing ship

This can be cut from a single square of felt by cutting it as shown (Fig 7), but it is more interesting if different colours are used. Sew the boat shape near the bottom edge of the square. From the middle of it embroider a mast in black chain or stem stitch and arrange the sails one each side of it.

A Christmas tree

Cut this out of green felt freely without a pattern because the sides do not have to match (Fig 8).

A yellow felt rabbit

Draw this from two circles, the smaller one for the head overlapping on to the larger body one (Fig 9). Add the ears and trace on to the felt. The fluffy tail is made from white silky wool sewn over and over in loops which are cut and trimmed. Embroider the whiskers in yellow cotton.

A teapot

is a circle with a piece cut off at the bottom to make it straight, and a handle, spout and knob added. Cut it out in one piece and sew on (Fig 10).

Assembly of the cube

When all the squares are embroidered, sew four of them round one with all the right sides on top. Make a box by sewing the sides together, keeping the right sides outside (Fig 11). Sew on the remaining piece like a lid, leaving two sides unsewn. Push small pieces of kapok gently into the corners and seams, using a blunt pencil. Sew up the remaining two sides, pushing in any extra stuffing as you go.

An alphabet cube

The pictured cube has green letters on a yellow cube and is 8 cm (3") square, the letters being 4 cm (1½") (Fig 12). Choose colours which contrast well so that they stand out boldly. Sew each letter into the middle of a square and arrange the squares in any order. When sewing up be careful to keep the right sides outside. Finish off like the dice.

A number cube

This one in bright orange felt with dark brown numbers is a 10 cm (4") cube.

You will need:

A piece of felt 20 cm by 31 cm (8" by 12"); or each square could be a different colour; contrasting felt; matching cottons.

Cut out six 10 cm (4") squares. If fabric is used it should be very firm in weave and each square should measure 13 cm (5") (Fig 13), allowing 1.25 cm (½") each side for turnings.

The figures are 5 cm (2") long (Fig 14). Use a good contrast for them. Sew a figure in the middle of each square and finish off the cube like the dice.

Solid bricks

Bricks in different sizes and colours are another favourite toy with young children, and are quite simple to make.

You will need:

For a 10 cm (4") brick a thick piece of card measuring 31 cm by 40 cm (12" by 16") and six squares of felt each measuring 10.3 cm (4⅛") square (the extra 3 mm (⅛") on the felt allows both for the thickness of the card and for the sewing up); matching cotton; masking tape.

Mark the card in 10 cm (4") squares (Fig 15) and cut away the shaded parts. Score across the dotted lines with a sharp penknife and bend the squares carefully away from the cuts (Fig 16). Form it into a cube and stick masking tape along all the edges to seal and strengthen them.

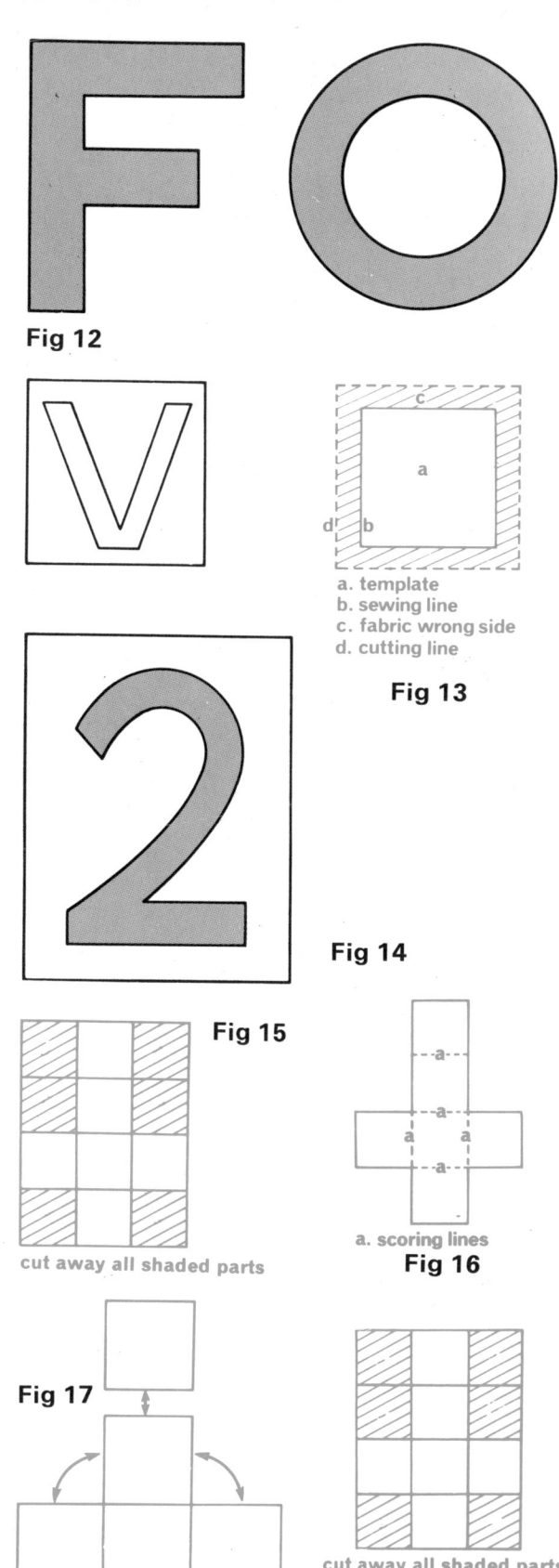

Fig 12

a. template
b. sewing line
c. fabric wrong side
d. cutting line

Fig 13

Fig 14

Fig 15

cut away all shaded parts

a. scoring lines
Fig 16

Fig 17

Fig 18

cut away all shaded parts

27

Sew four felt squares round one square making a cross (Fig 17), and sew their sides together to make a box. Sew on one side of the remaining square to make a lid. Slide the card cube into the felt box and sew down the three remaining sides.

Make a set of bricks by cutting the squares 1 cm ($\frac{1}{2}$") smaller for each brick. The process of making is the same for any size brick. Very gay bricks can be made by using different-coloured felts for each side.

The shaped card for the brick can be used as a template on the felt to cut out the felt shape in one piece instead of separate squares (Fig 18). This gives a box with less joins. Care must be taken to allow a margin all round the traced shape to allow for the thickness of the card.

An oblong brick

For an oblong brick measuring 15 cm by 8 cm by 4 cm (6" by 3" by 1$\frac{1}{2}$").

You will need:

A piece of card 23 cm (9") square; a 24 cm (9$\frac{1}{2}$") square of felt; some masking tape; matching sewing cotton.

Mark the card and cut away the shaded portions (Fig 19). The card can be used as a template for cutting the felt shape, leaving a margin of about 3 mm ($\frac{1}{8}$") all round the shape for sewing up and the thickness of the card.

Oversew the four pairs of short sides together to form a box shape with a lid.

Score along the dotted lines on the card (Fig 20) and carefully bend the sides away from the cuts. Form into a brick and bind every side with masking tape. Slide the brick into the felt box and sew down the lid.

As an alternative, a more tailored, neater brick is obtained by cutting separate pieces of felt for top, base and sides.

For this you will need to cut pieces of felt:

Two pieces 15.3 cm by 8.3 cm (6$\frac{1}{8}$" by 3$\frac{1}{8}$") for the top and the base.
Two pieces 15.3 cm by 4.3 cm (6$\frac{1}{8}$" by 1$\frac{5}{8}$") for the long sides.
Two pieces 8.3 cm by 4.3 cm (3$\frac{1}{8}$" by 1$\frac{5}{8}$") for the short sides.

Join a long side piece to the long sides on the base, and similarly the short sides. The rest of the making up is the same.

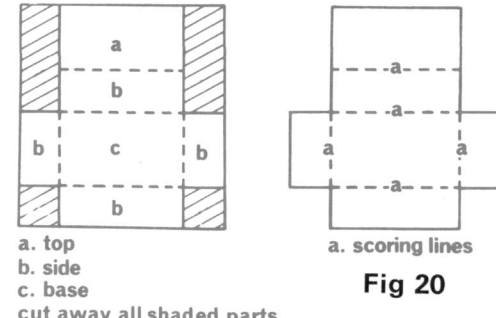

a. top
b. side
c. base
cut away all shaded parts

Fig 19

a. scoring lines

Fig 20

A pillar

This one in blue felt measures 15 cm by 2.5 cm by 2.5 cm (6" by 1" by 1").

You will need:

A piece of felt 11 cm by 21 cm (4$\frac{1}{2}$" by 8$\frac{1}{2}$"); a piece of thick card 10 cm by 20 cm (4" by 8"); masking tape; matching cotton.

Draw the shape on the card (Fig 21) and cut away the shaded parts. Use the card as a template for tracing the shape on to the felt, allowing 3 mm ($\frac{1}{8}$") for thickness of the card (Fig 22). If you wish to make it up in separate pieces, you will need four pieces 15.3 cm by 3 cm (6$\frac{1}{8}$" by 1$\frac{1}{8}$") and 2 pieces 3 cm (1$\frac{1}{8}$") square. Make it up in the same way as the oblong brick.

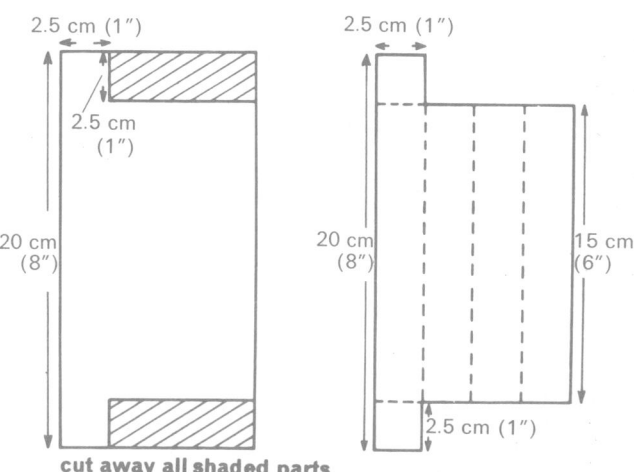

cut away all shaded parts

Fig 21   **Fig 22**

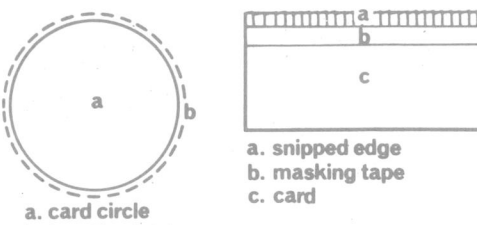

a. card circle
b. length of strip

Fig 23

a. snipped edge
b. masking tape
c. card

Fig 24

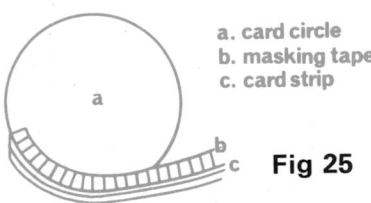

a. card circle
b. masking tape
c. card strip

Fig 25

A drum shape

The shape is made up from two circles and a long strip long enough to go right round the circles (Fig 23). Different sizes can be made by varying the size of the circles and the width of the strip.

You will need:

Card, not too thick; felt; masking tape; matching cotton.

Use the cards as templates to trace the felt shape, cutting them 3 mm ($\frac{1}{8}$") bigger all round.

Oversew one edge of the felt strip to the felt circle and join the ends of the strip. Stick masking tape all along one long edge of the card strip, using half the width of the tape, leaving the other half-width free. Snip this free width into a fringe, taking the cuts up to the edge of the card (Fig 24). Place the edge of the circle to the edge of the strip and stick the fringed masking tape on to it, bending the long card as you go to follow the curve of the circle (Fig 25). Repeat this with the second card circle. Slide this drum into the felt shape and sew the remaining felt circle on top.

A cylinder

This is the same design as the drum, the circles being smaller and the long strip wider. The making up is the same. Long pillars are made with 2.5 cm (1") diameter circles and 15 cm (6") wide strips, to match the square pillars already described.

A pyramid

To make one in pink felt on an 8 cm (3") square base.

You will need:

A piece of card 23 cm (9") square; felt 24 cm ($9\frac{1}{2}$") square; masking tape; cotton matching the felt.

Mark the card into 8 cm (3") squares and mark the centre of each side of the square. Join these centre points to each corner of the middle 8 cm (3") square (Fig 26). Cut away the shaded parts.

Trace your felt shape from this template allowing the extra 3 mm ($\frac{1}{8}$") all round (Fig 27). Score along the sides of the centre card square and bend the triangular shapes away from the cuts, so forming a pyramid. Bind all the edges with masking tape.

Oversew the sides of three of the felt triangles, slide the card pyramid inside and sew up the remaining triangle.

A solid triangle

This shape is easier to handle if both card shape and felt can be cut out in one piece (Fig 28).

You will need:

Thin card about 40 cm by 18 cm (16" by 7"); felt 6 mm ($\frac{1}{4}$") larger; masking tape; matching sewing cotton.

Draw an inch-wide strip across the middle of the length of card; mark a 15 cm (6") line in the middle. Draw a right-angled triangle on this base on both sides of the strip (Fig 29).

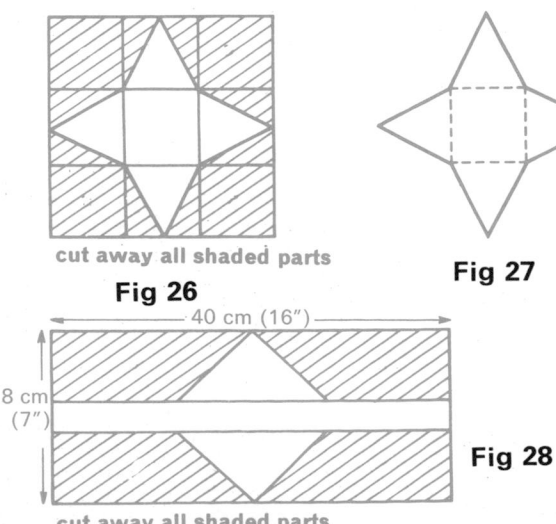

cut away all shaded parts

Fig 26

Fig 27

cut away all shaded parts

Fig 28

Trace from this template on to the felt, allowing an extra 3 mm ($\frac{1}{8}''$) all round. Score the sides of the base of the card rectangle, bending carefully away from the cuts. Bind all the edges together with masking tape.

Sew one strip at one side of the triangle to both sides of the triangle, slide in the card shape, and sew the second strip to the other sides of the triangle.

Various sizes can be made in this shape by altering the measurements of the triangle.

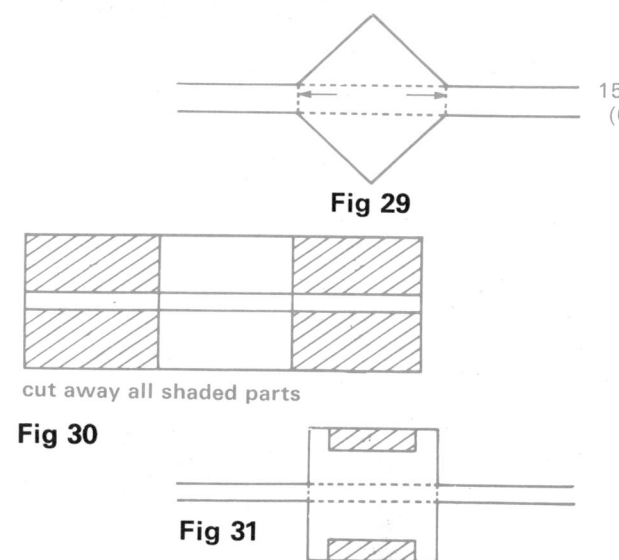

Fig 29

cut away all shaded parts

Fig 30

Fig 31

A square arch

You will need:

Felt; card; masking tape; sewing cotton. The pictured arch measures 10 cm by 5 cm by 2.5 cm (4" by 2" by 1"). The size of felt needed is 37 cm by 13 cm ($14\frac{1}{4}''$ by $5\frac{1}{4}''$) and the card 36 cm by 13 cm (14" by 5").

Draw a cross in the middle of the card with the upright 10 cm (4") wide and the horizontal cross piece 2.5 cm (1") wide (Fig 30). Cut away the shaded parts as shown. Draw a rectangle at each end of the upright measuring 5 cm by 2.5 cm (2" by 1"). Cut away these rectangles (Fig 31).

Use this card as a template to cut the felt shape, allowing 3 mm ($\frac{1}{8}''$) extra all round. A smaller piece of felt measuring 13 cm by 16 cm ($5\frac{1}{4}''$ by $6\frac{1}{2}''$) can be used for the felt shape if the long side strips are sewn on separately (Fig 32).

From this piece of felt cut two strips measuring 13 cm by 2.5 cm ($5\frac{1}{4}''$ by 1") leaving a rectangle 13 cm by 10 cm ($5\frac{1}{4}''$ by $4\frac{1}{4}''$).

Cut the arch shape from this piece and sew on a long strip at each side as shown, to make the required shape. Score all the dotted lines on the card and bend the sections away from the cuts, thus forming the arch. Bind all the edges with masking tape.

To make the felt cover

Sew one long side of the 2.5 cm (1") strips of felt to one half of the arch so that the joining up of the ends of the strips comes in the centre of the under side of the arch. Slide in the card shape and sew the other side of the strip to the other side of

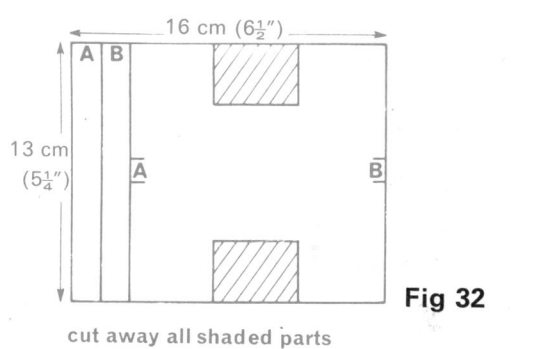

Fig 32

cut away all shaded parts

the arch, taking care to match up the corners with the first side.

A semi-circular arch

You will need:

Card; felt, about 20 cm by 16 cm (8" by $6\frac{1}{2}''$); masking tape; cotton.

On the card draw a semi-circle on a 13 cm (5") diameter and a second one inside on an 8 cm (3") diameter (Fig 33). Cut round both arcs. Trace round this arch for the second side and extend the ends for an inch each side (Fig 34). Cut two strips of card 20 cm by 2.5 cm (8" by 1") and 10 cm by 2.5 cm (4" by 1"). Use these

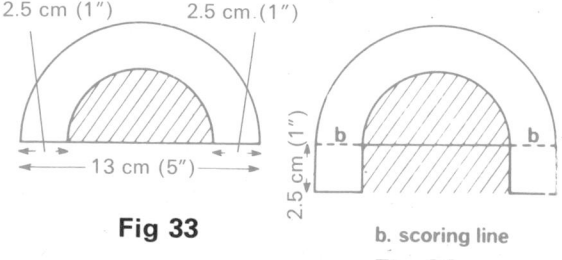

Fig 33

b. scoring line

Fig 34

cards as templates to cut the felt shapes allowing 3 mm ($\frac{1}{8}$") extra (Fig 35).

To make up the card arch, score across the dotted lines at the base of the larger arch and bend them away from the cuts until they are at right angles to the arch. Stick masking tape along one side of the long strip using half the width of tape, snip the edges of the other half-width of tape and stick it on to the outer curve of the arch, bending the card gently to fit the curve. If each cut piece of masking tape is pressed down in turn, it will help to bend the strip into place.

Repeat this with the shorter strip on the shorter curve on the same arch. Join on the second side of the arch in the same way and then bind with tape the edges of the base of the arch.

Mark 2.5 cm (1") from each end of the long strip of felt and pin the centre part to the outer curve of a semi-circular piece.

Oversew the edges, and sew the remaining inch each side along the edge of the base.

Repeat this with the shorter strip on the same arch, again sewing the remaining inch each side to the base. Sew the smaller curve of the second arch on to the strip. Slide the card arch inside the felt and sew up the long curve.

Many sizes can be made but very small ones are difficult to sew on the inner curve.

Hollow bricks

There are six of these in bright-coloured felt, the largest one 13 cm (5") and the smallest 3 cm (1$\frac{1}{4}$"), each one 2 cm ($\frac{3}{4}$") smaller. Each brick needs five squares of card and ten squares of felt. Sizes of felt needed to cut these squares for each size are:

63 cm by 26 cm (25$\frac{5}{8}$" by 10$\frac{1}{4}$") for the largest,
55 cm by 21 cm (21$\frac{7}{8}$" by 8$\frac{3}{4}$"),
47 cm by 18 cm (18$\frac{1}{8}$" by 7$\frac{1}{4}$"),
36 cm by 13 cm (14$\frac{3}{8}$" by 5$\frac{3}{4}$"),
26 cm by 10 cm (10$\frac{5}{8}$" by 4$\frac{1}{4}$"),
16 cm by 6 cm (6$\frac{7}{8}$" by 2$\frac{3}{4}$").

Cards needed are
Five 13 cm (5") squares,
Five 10 cm (4$\frac{1}{4}$"),
Five 9 cm (3$\frac{1}{2}$"),
Five 6 cm (2$\frac{3}{4}$"),
Five 5 cm (2"),
Five 3 cm (1$\frac{1}{4}$")

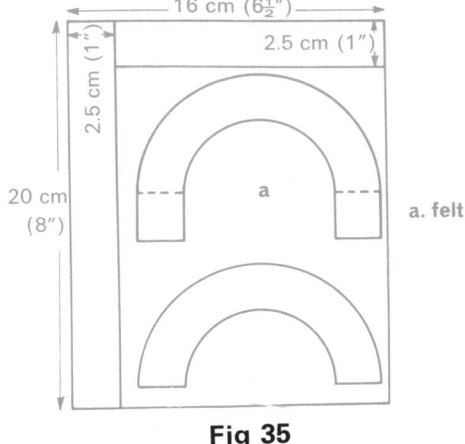

Fig 35

a. felt

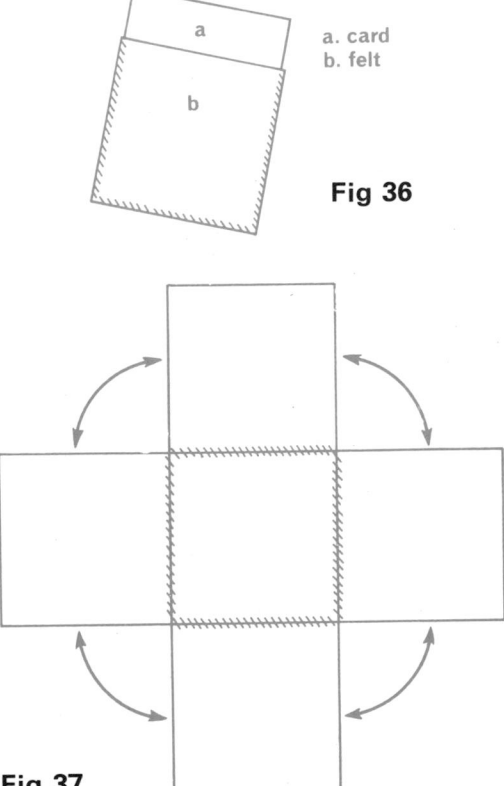

a. card
b. felt

Fig 36

Fig 37

It is wise to cut the largest squares first.

Beginning with the largest brick, cut ten pieces of felt in squares measuring 13 cm (5$\frac{1}{8}$"). Join them together in twos by oversewing the edges on three sides, keeping the pencil-marked edges inside. Slide a card inside the felt pocket and oversew remaining edges (Fig 36). When all five squares are sewn, sew four squares round one square. Form into a box by sewing together the sides of these four squares (Fig 37). Repeat this with each of the other five bricks.

Mosaic tiles

Mosaic tiles of many shapes can be arranged in hundreds of different patterns and designs, both simple and intricate. These have provided a fascinating pastime for many years; perhaps since the Italians began hundreds of years ago with small squares of coloured stone and glass to beautify ceilings, walls and floors in houses and temples. Those in Ravenna are still glorious today.

The shapes here are easy to handle, being felt- or material-covered card, and will make an endless number of designs, especially if they are planned on one unit or multiples of one unit. For instance, a number of 8 cm (3″) squares can be cut into halves and quarters, and thirds, in several ways, or can be used with 15 cm (6″) squares and still fit into quite intricate patterns. Squares of different sizes will not fit together so satisfactorily.

You will need:

Fairly thick card; felt; sewing cotton.

Cut ten 8 cm (3″) squares of card. Leave five of them as squares and cut the others (Fig 38). Using a square as a template, trace and cut out two squares of felt measuring 8.3 cm ($3\frac{1}{8}$″) to allow for the thickness of the card. Place the two felts together and oversew round three sides. Slide the card into the felt pocket and oversew the remaining edges. Repeat this with the other squares and then with the other shapes.

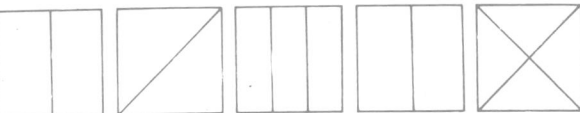

Fig 38

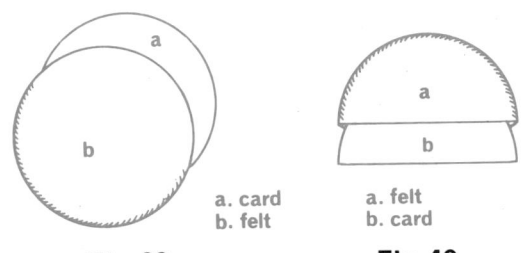

a. card
b. felt

Fig 39

a. felt
b. card

Fig 40

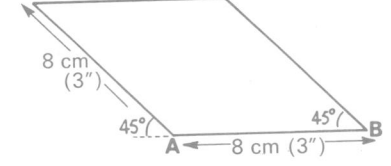

8 cm
(3″)

45° 45°
A 8 cm (3″) B

Fig 41

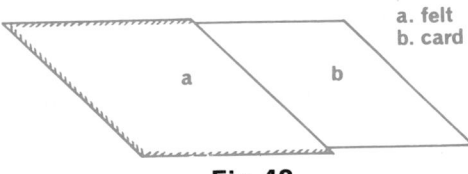

a. felt
b. card

Fig 42

Circular tiles

Draw four circles of 8 cm (3″) diameter. Cut one circle in half and another one in quarters. Cut two felt shapes 3 mm ($\frac{1}{8}$″) larger for each of the shapes.

Sew the felt circles together halfway round, slide in the card and sew up the opening (Fig 39). For the semi-circles, join the curved sides and slide in the cards (Fig 40); join any two sides in the quarter-circles first, slide in the cards and sew up the opening.

Diamond shapes

Cut diamond shapes by using a protractor or the angle section on a ruler. Draw a line 8 cm (3″) long (AB in Fig 41). Place the ruler along the line with the 90° line on it at A and mark with a dot where the 45° line points to the left. Join A to the dot and make the line 8 cm (3″) long. Repeat this at B. Join up the ends of the line to make the diamond shape. Cover this with felt in the same way (Fig 42).

Alphabet tiles

These and matching symbol pictures can be made in the same way as the mosaic tiles with card inserts or with an insert of interlining which makes them much softer to handle.

You will need:

Various colours of felt (small pieces will do for the pictures); some fairly thick interlining or wadding; matching cotton; thin card for templates. For a 10 cm (4") tile you need a piece of felt 10 cm by 20 cm (4" by 8") cut generously.

Cut felt in half. Cut out in card a letter measuring 5 cm (2") and trace it on to a piece of contrasting felt. Cut it out and sew it in the middle of one square. Place the squares together with the right sides outside and sew round three sides.

Cut a piece of interlining or wadding slightly less than 10 cm (4") square (cut a double piece if it is thin) and insert it in the felt pocket, smoothing it into the corners. Sew up the remaining side.

To make a matching symbol tile, for instance a cup for letter 'C' (Fig 43), draw a simple silhouette of a cup on thin card and cut it out, use as a template and trace off on contrasting felt.

Sew the symbol on one square and make it up in the same way as the first tile. A series of number tiles and matching symbol pictures or dots can be made in the same way (Fig 44).

Letters and numbers

These are soft to handle and easy for small fingers to grasp. They can be made flat from two pieces or rounder and fatter by inserting a straight gusset all round. The pictured letters (Fig 45), are 13 cm (5") long and most of them 10 cm (4") wide.

You will need:

Various colours of felt — each side of the letter can be different; thin card for templates; kapok or similar; matching cotton.

Plan the letters or numbers in a rectangle 13 cm by 10 cm (5" by 4") making the lines or curves of the letter 2.5 cm (1") wide (Fig 46). Make templates, trace round these shapes on to the felt and cut them out. Place the pieces together with right sides outside and oversew.

Oversewing must be planned, because in many cases stuffing must be done at the same time.

Letter 'D' — sew the inner curves first, then stuff as you sew the outer edges.

Letter 'R' — sew inner curve and inner edge of uprights. Oversew outer edge stuffing as you go.

Letter 'P' — similar to D.

Letter 'E' — similar to R.

Letter 'A' — sew inner triangle and inner edges of legs. Sew outer edges, filling with stuffing.

Figure 6 — sew inner edges. Sew outer edges starting at the top and stuff in small sections round the curve.

Figure 8 — sew the two inner edges. Sew the outer edges in very small sections and stuff. Be careful not to pull the stitches when stuffing.

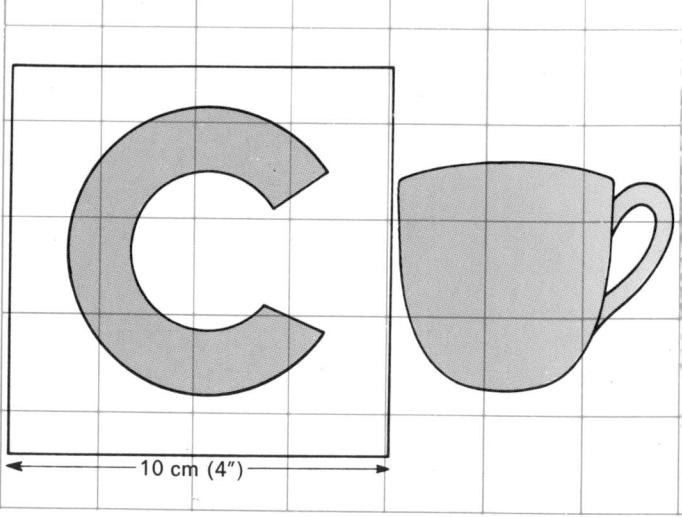

Fig 43

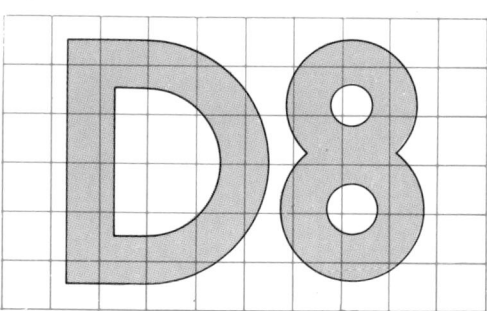

Fig 45

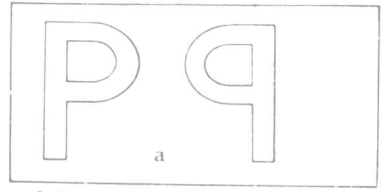

a. felt

Fig 46

Fig 44

39

CHAPTER THREE

Puppets

Puppets can be very simple or very elaborate, with all the stages in between. They progress from the early experimental ones made by young children for immediate use and with bare essentials; they will use their own imagination to clothe the puppet as princess or clown, witch or dragon. These are made from homely materials, easily obtained, such as cardboard picnic plates, cheese boxes, margarine cartons, cream and yogurt cartons, or cardboard tubes. Some of them can be mounted on sticks for easy handling.

Others demand more skill in their making, involving cutting out from a pattern, sewing them and adding details of clothing and decoration to determine their character. Again, more sophisticated ones are made of craft materials like clay, wood, wire, papier mâché and potter's plaster, using new techniques with new tools – carving, moulding, sculpting.

Most children enjoy using puppets and often the shy, withdrawn child will become talkative and quite eloquent when it is *his* puppet who is seen and heard while he himself is safely out of sight and quite anonymous behind his screen.

Glove puppets – basic shapes

Two basic shapes are used here which can be adapted in many ways to give a great variety of characters. Most of the animals can be made – as well as fabulous creatures and monsters, space people, everyday policemen, soldiers, sailors, nursery-rhyme and story characters, people from history and people from other lands. Both shapes are glove puppets, one with a mouth and the other with arms.

Puppets with a mouth

Any materials can be used, but an allowance for seams and a hem must be added to the pattern if the material is likely to fray. Felt or Vilene are some of the easiest ones to use because they do not fray when they are cut.

The template

The template shape is an oblong with one rounded end. Individual ones can be made by drawing round your hand placed flat on a piece of card with thumb close to the fingers, from the wrist on one side, round the fingers to the other side of the wrist (Fig 1a). Leave an extra allowance all round to allow for the thickness of your

hand and extra again when cutting out the fabric to allow for movement of the fingers when using the puppet. It should look like (Fig 1b).

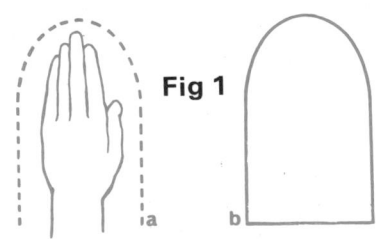

Fig 1

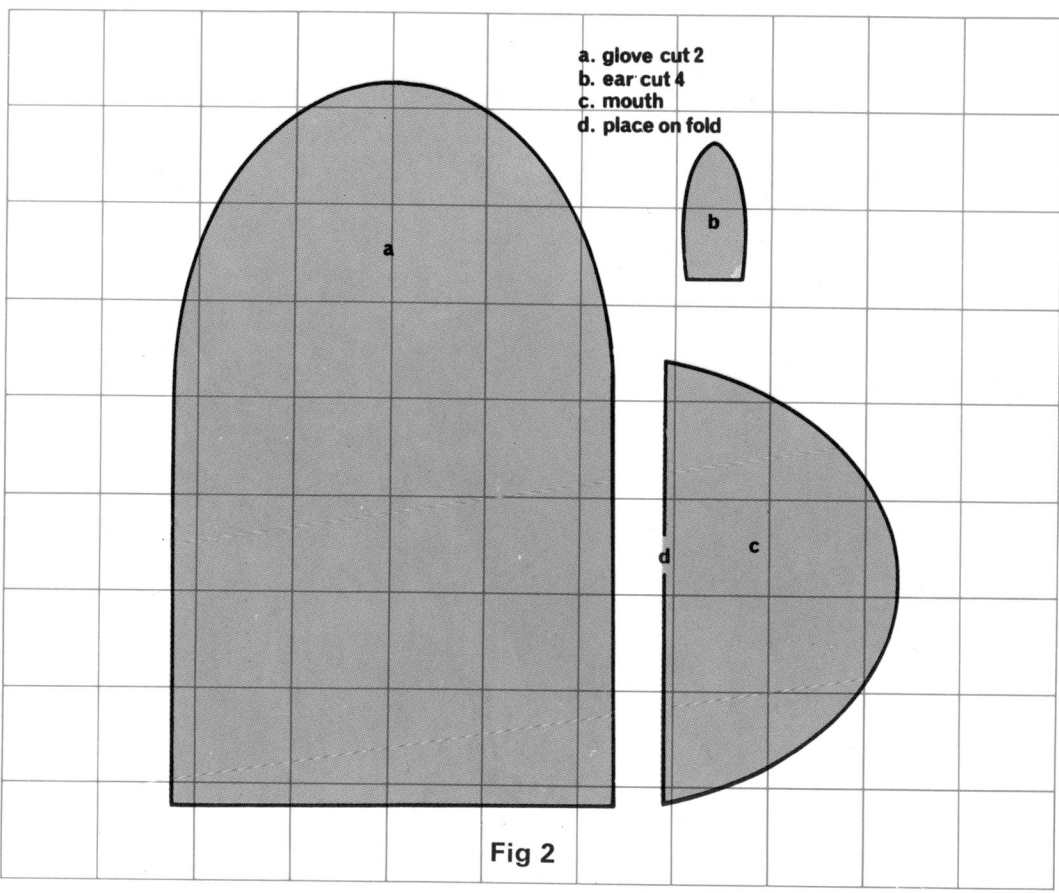

a. glove cut 2
b. ear cut 4
c. mouth
d. place on fold

a

b

d   c

Fig 2

A rabbit

This rabbit is just a head with a mouth, which is worked with one hand. Your thumb fits into the lower half of the mouth and fingers into the upper half. You can make dozens of different 'faces' by opening and closing your fingers and thumb, and by clenching them and twisting them so that the rabbit seems to be talking and laughing. This one is made from fluffy, white man-made fibre, the kind which is often used to make warm dressing gowns; it is pictures on p 60.

You will need:

A hand's length of fluffy man-made fibre measuring from just below your wrist to your fingertips and the width to go right round the thickest part of your hand (Fig 2). (Allow an inch or so extra on the width to give room for movement and an extra 5 cm (2") on the length to use for the long ears); a piece of pinky-orange felt for the inside of the mouth; some strands of black and pink embroidery silk; a little narrow ribbon bow, and a pattern.

Cut out the felt

Lay your template on the material and cut two pieces, remembering to allow the little extra for movement. The ears template is shaped like a pointed arch and its length should be a little more than half the width of your hand. Cut four pieces from the pattern (Fig 3).

Make another template for the mouth by drawing round the top of the hand template from where it begins to curve. Place this on the folded pink felt, with the straight edge of the template on the fold (Fig 4).

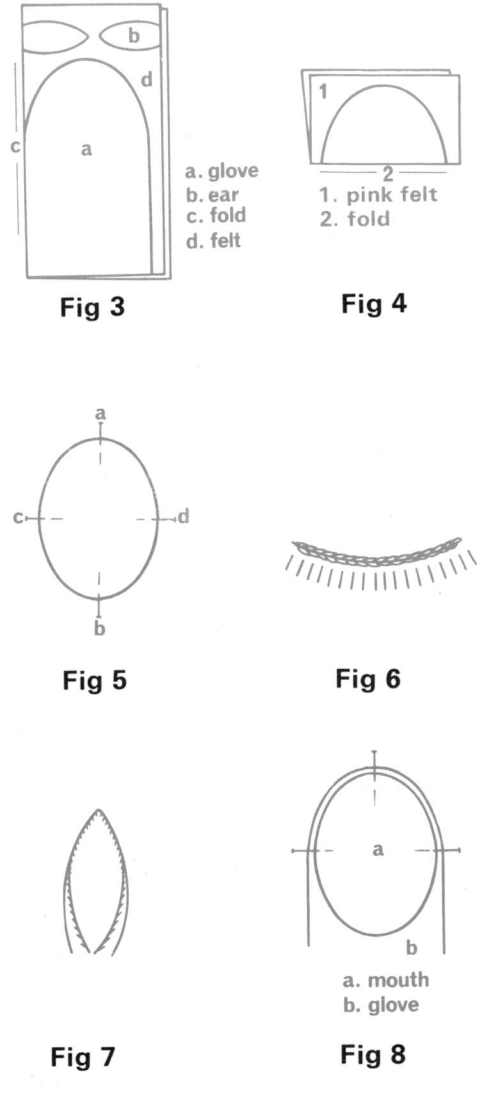

Fig 3

a. glove
b. ear
c. fold
d. felt

Fig 4

1. pink felt
2. fold

Fig 5

Fig 6

Fig 7

Fig 8

a. mouth
b. glove

Cut it out. Mark the fold at each end with a pin. Fold it in half the other way and mark each end with a pin so that it is in quarters (Fig 5).

Features

Embroider the features on to one piece of man-made fibre, being careful to make them look towards the curve. Fold the piece in half lengthways to find the middle of the curve. Embroider a nostril each side of this point by working four little straight stitches close together in pink silk. For the closed eyes draw two curves in pencil and work a line of chain stitch in black embroidery silk, and underneath it a line of straight stitches for eyelashes (Fig 6).

Place two ear pieces together with right sides outside and oversew the two edges closely together, leaving the straight edge which is the bottom of the ear. Fold the two corners to the centre of the straight edge and stitch down (Fig 7). Repeat for the second ear. Sew them in place just above the eyes, with the fold facing forward. Sew them down across the front, and then bend them forward and sew across the back. This double stitching will help to make them stand up.

Now pin point 'a' on the pink felt to the centre of the face curve, between the two nostrils, and pin 'c' and 'd' to either side. Sew this half of the mouth to the face with tiny stitches. Find the centre of the back glove piece and to it pin point 'b' on the mouth and similarly 'c' and 'd', and stitch this in place (Figs 5 and 8). Close the mouth so that the upper and lower parts fit over each other and oversew the glove seams from points 'e' and 'd' to the wrist (Fig 9). Sew the little ribbon bow between the ears and your puppet is ready.

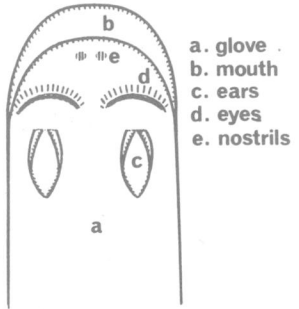

a. glove
b. mouth
c. ears
d. eyes
e. nostrils

Fig 9

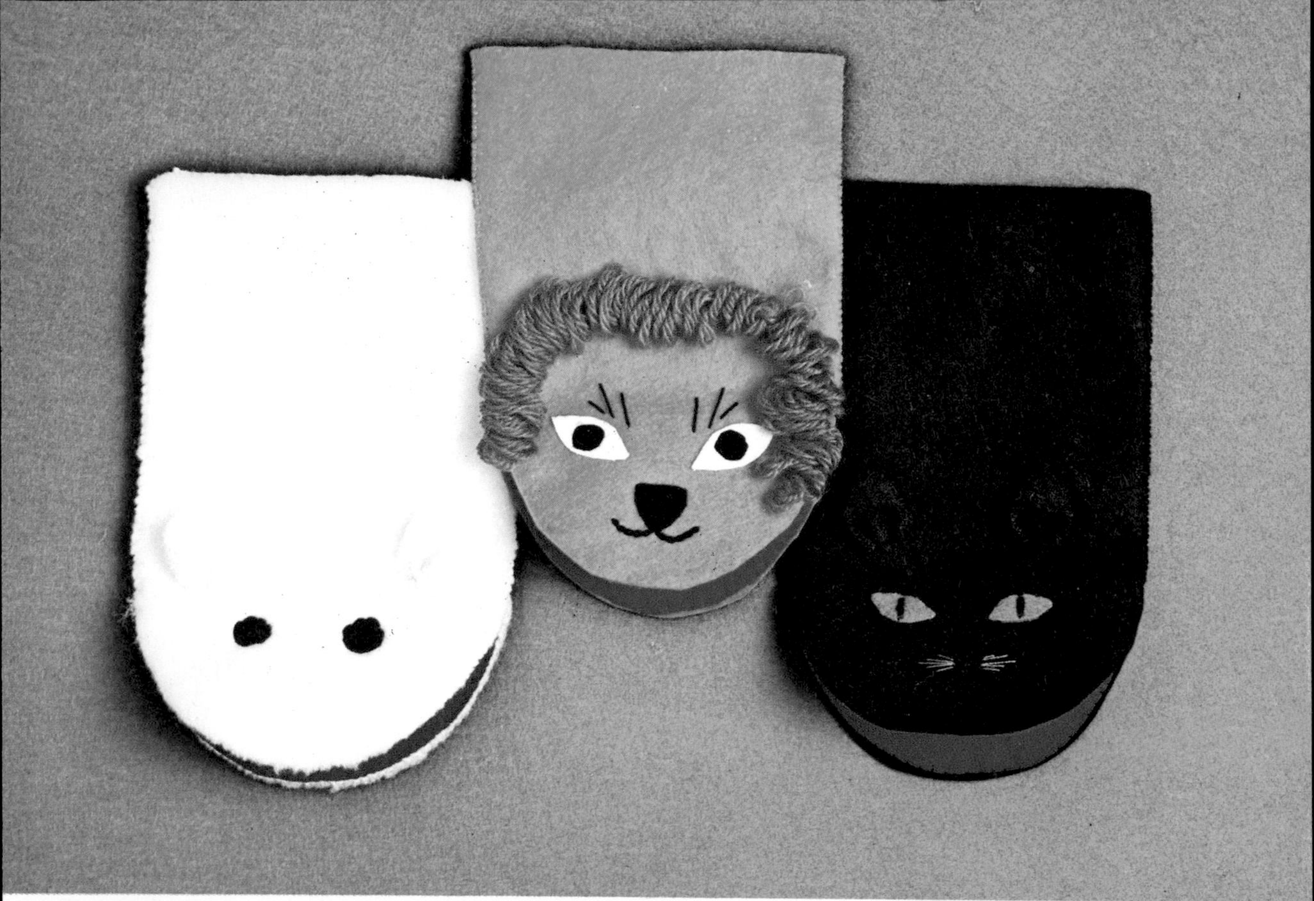

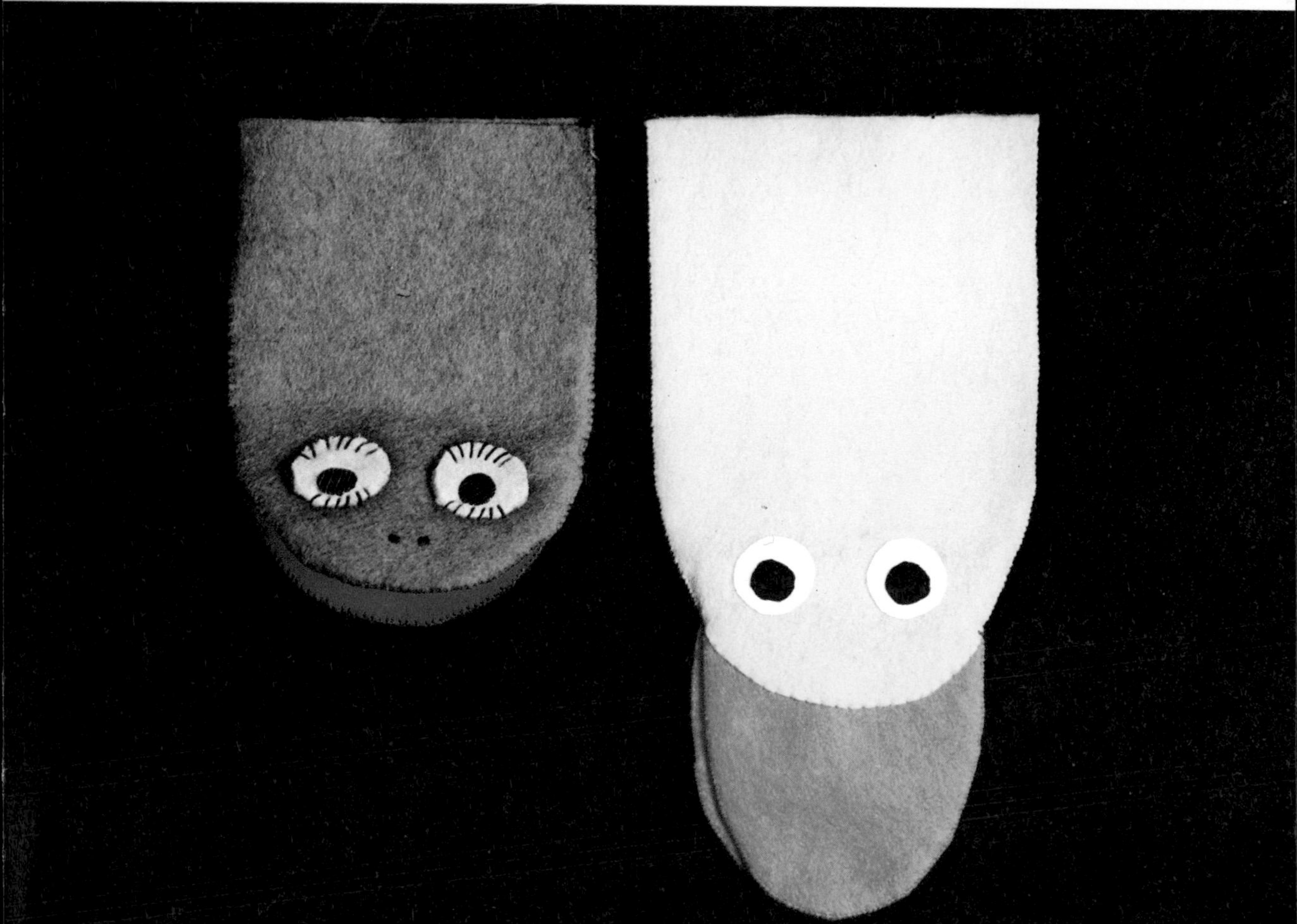

A lamb

This can also be made in fluffy white man-made fibre or in white felt. A little less material is needed because it has no ears included in the pattern. Make it up in the same way as the rabbit.

A frog

For this simple type of puppet use bright, grass-green felt with an orange inner mouth. Cut large circles in white inter-lining material or white felt for the eyes, with large sequin centres (Fig 10), or circles of card covered with fine, glittering metal-thread material, fastened down with long straight stitches in black above and below the circles. Make up as the rabbit.

a. sequin
b. white felt

Fig 10

A lion

The lion is made in orange felt with a scarlet mouth, some tawny-coloured wool for a mane and scraps of black felt for features. Cut a small oval shape in black felt for a nose (Fig 11) and sew it on in the centre of the rounded end about an inch away from the edge. Embroider the mouth in black embroidery silk. For the eyes cut two ovals pointed at each end in white or pale yellow felt, sew a circle of black felt in the middle of each (Fig 12) and sew them above the nose at an angle, slanting towards the nose, with three or four straight stitches above them for brows. Sew loops of wool closely together all round the top and sides of the face for his mane (Fig 13). Finish the making up in the same way as the rabbit.

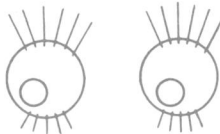

Fig 14

Fig 15

A schoolgirl

You will need:

Natural-coloured or flesh felt for the head; a pink or red felt mouth; scraps of blue and white felt for her eyes; brown or blonde wool for her hair; some ribbon for bows.

Two small straight stitch spots are sewn for her nose each side of the centre of the curve. The eyes are exaggerated in size to give a rather comical-looking face. Cut two large circles in white felt with two smaller circles in blue placed on to one side and near the bottom of them to give her a sideways glance (Fig 14). Fasten them to the face with large stitches at the top and bottom for eyelashes. Cut about 20 strands of wool 20 cm (8") long. Lay them across the head above the eyes and sew them down the centre with back stitch to simulate a parting. Catch them down at each side of the face and sew on a ribbon bow at each side (Fig 15). The strands of wool can be cut longer than 20 cm (8") if liked and the ends plaited instead. Make up as for the rabbit.

A duck

You will need:

Yellow felt for the head; red felt for the mouth; bright orange felt for the

Fig 11   **Fig 12**   **Fig 13**

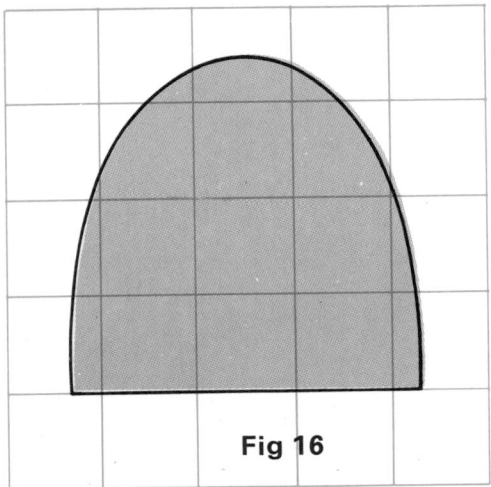

Fig 16

(Fig 18). The stages for making it are the same as for the duck, and you can see the finished result on page 60, together with the brown bear (*see* below).

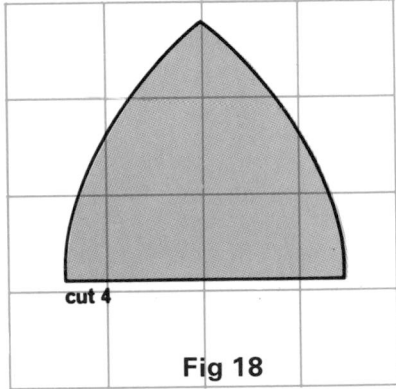

cut 4

Fig 18

beak; white and black felt pieces for the eyes.

The template for the beak is a smaller version of the puppet template (Fig 16).

Cut four pieces of orange felt for the beak. Join them together in pairs, over-sewing round the curved edge (Fig 17).

Cut out two circles of white·felt with black circles in the centre for eyes and sew them in position.

Place the straight edge of the beak under the curved end of the face piece and sew down round the curved end with small, invisible stitches which are taken through only one thickness of the beak.

Match the position of the other beak on the other half of the puppet and sew on similarly. Finish the making up as for the rabbit.

A chick

This is similar to the duck in most respects except that the beak is pointed at the end

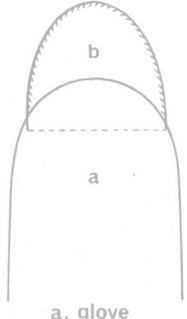

b

a

Fig 17

a. glove
b. beak

A brown/polar bear

You will need:

Brown or fawn felt for a brown bear; white fluffy man-made fibre or white felt for a little polar bear; black and white felt; black embroidery silk.

Cut four pieces from the ear template (Fig 19) and join them in twos for each ear by oversewing the curved edges to-gether. Cut a small shield shape in black felt for a nose, sew it in place and em-broider the mouth underneath it in black embroidery silk. Sew two small circles in white felt with black felt centres on for eyes. (Cut slightly larger black felt circles for the polar bear and omit the white circles.)

Fold the corners of the ears to the centre and sew on the face with ladder stitch (Fig 20), taking a stitch in the ear and a stitch in the face, sewing all round both at front and back; this will make the ears stand up. Making up is the same as for the rabbit.

Fig 19   **Fig 20**

Fig 21 (actual size)

A cat

This is made in black, grey or ginger-coloured felt. Two pointed ears similar in shape but smaller than those on the rabbit, are added (Fig 21), a nose like the bear's, and green embroidery silk or fine metal-thread whiskers embroidered each side of it (Fig 22). A pair of green felt oval eyes, slanted in to the nose and fastened down with an upright stitch like a bar in black silk, finishes the features.

Cut four pieces of felt for the ears. Oversew the curved edges of two pieces together for each ear, fold the corners in to the centre and sew on to the face on both sides of the ear with ladder stitch. Make up the remainder as for the rabbit.

Fig 22

A snake

You will need:

A slightly different shape of template. the rounded end becomes more pointed, rather like a large-size rabbit's ear (Fig 23), the mouthpiece also having this shape; some sequins; fine metal-thread; an 8 cm (3″) length of pipe cleaner.

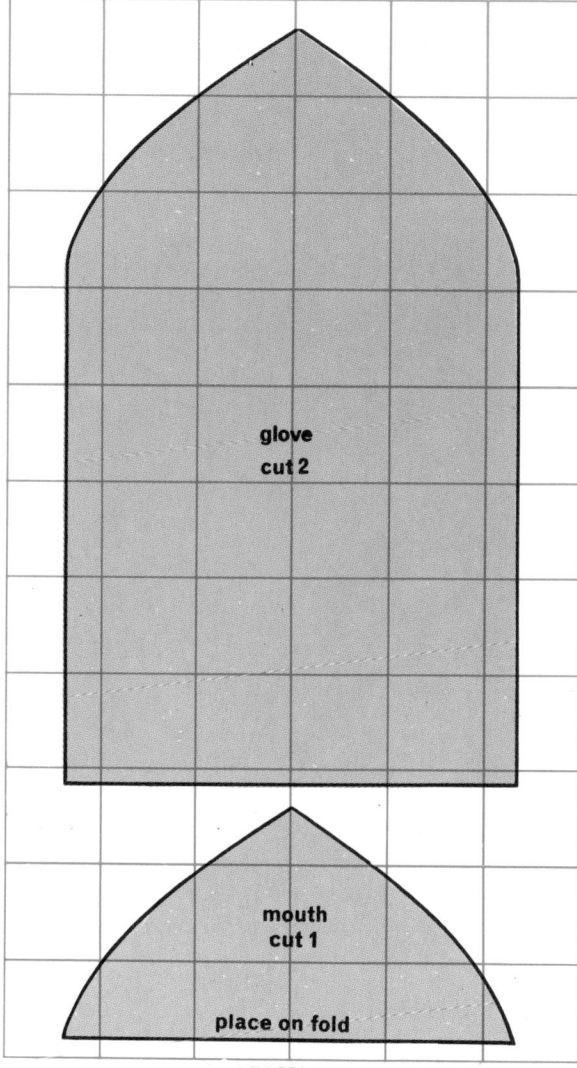

glove
cut 2

mouth
cut 1

place on fold

Fig 23

Cut two circles of black felt and embroider all round with straight stitches of fine red metal-thread and sew them on fairly close together.

Sew a band of red, green and gold sequins down the middle of the head, between the eyes, and spreading out into three or four lines at the mouth.

Bind the pipe cleaner closely with fine bright blue metal-thread, bend it into a V and sew it to the underside of the face piece as fangs. Make up like the rabbit.

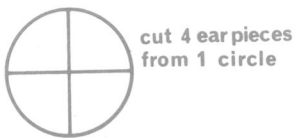

cut 4 ear pieces
from 1 circle

Fig 24

An elephant

You will need:

Dark grey felt for the body with a scarlet felt mouth; a 9 cm (3½″) circle of grey felt cut into four will make the ears (Fig 24); a 10 cm (4″) strip of grey felt 3.5 cm (1¾″) wide and narrowing off at one end for the trunk (Fig 25); a pipe cleaner twisted into a 10 cm (4″) length to stiffen the trunk.

Sew on two black circles for the eyes. Oversew two ear pieces all round for each ear and sew on by its corner above and to the side of the eyes. Oversew together the curved sides of the trunk, insert the pipe cleaner and pad softly with very small pieces of kapok. Sew on to the curve of the face with ladder stitch to make it stand away from the face. Complete the making like the rabbit.

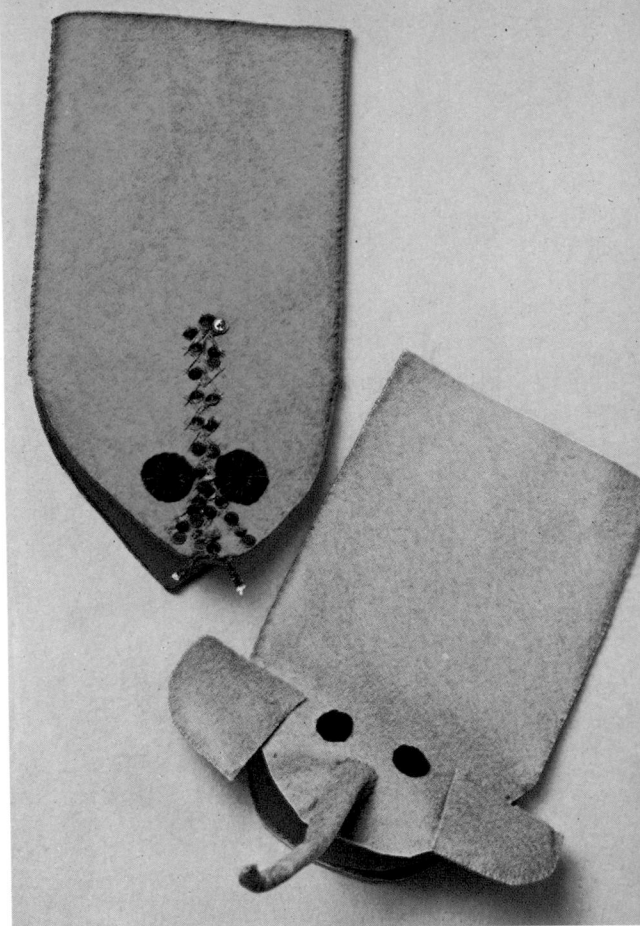

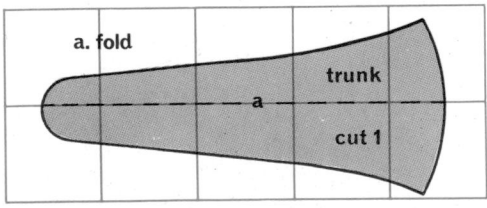

a. fold

trunk

a

cut 1

Fig 25

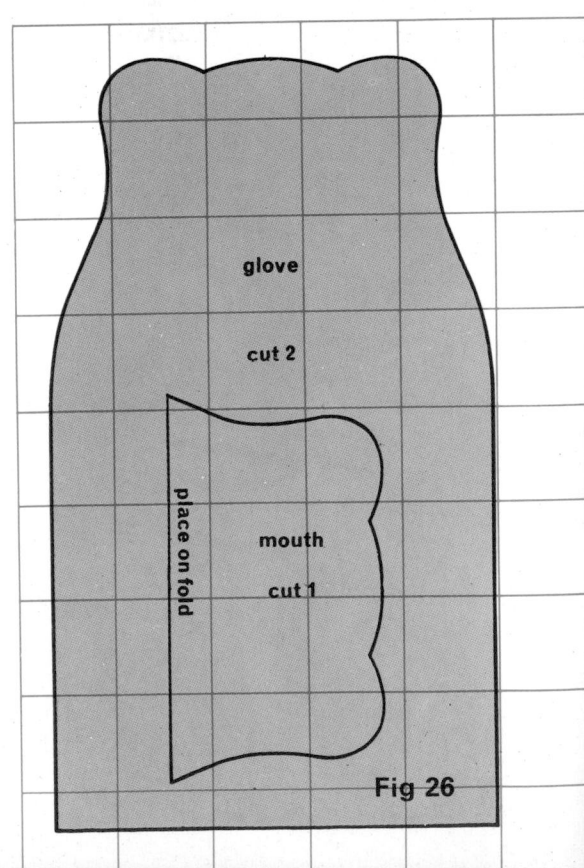

glove

cut 2

place on fold

mouth

cut 1

Fig 26

A dragon

You will need:

Bright green, orange, red felt; sequins; embroidery silk.

The rounded end of the template has again been altered to show a shaped snout with protuberant nostrils (Fig 26), and the inner mouth will naturally take the same outline. The mouth is lined with a bright orange felt — the dragon itself being in bright green — with a long, forked, red tongue (Fig 27) fastened at the fold at the back of the mouth and hanging out at the side.

The eyes are cut from bright orange felt with a large sequin or a ring of smaller sequins in the centre, sewn on at an angle slanting towards the nose. A line of chain stitch from the inner corners of them curves down and round each nostril. Sew a sequin in the nostril with a ring of chain stitch surrounding it (Fig 28).

A strip of red felt with one edge serrated is sewn down the back. Make up like the rabbit.

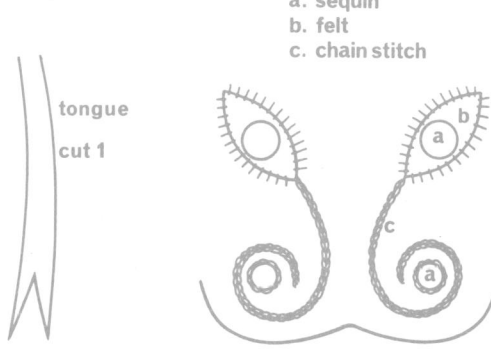

a. sequin
b. felt
c. chain stitch

tongue

cut 1

Fig 27   **Fig 28**

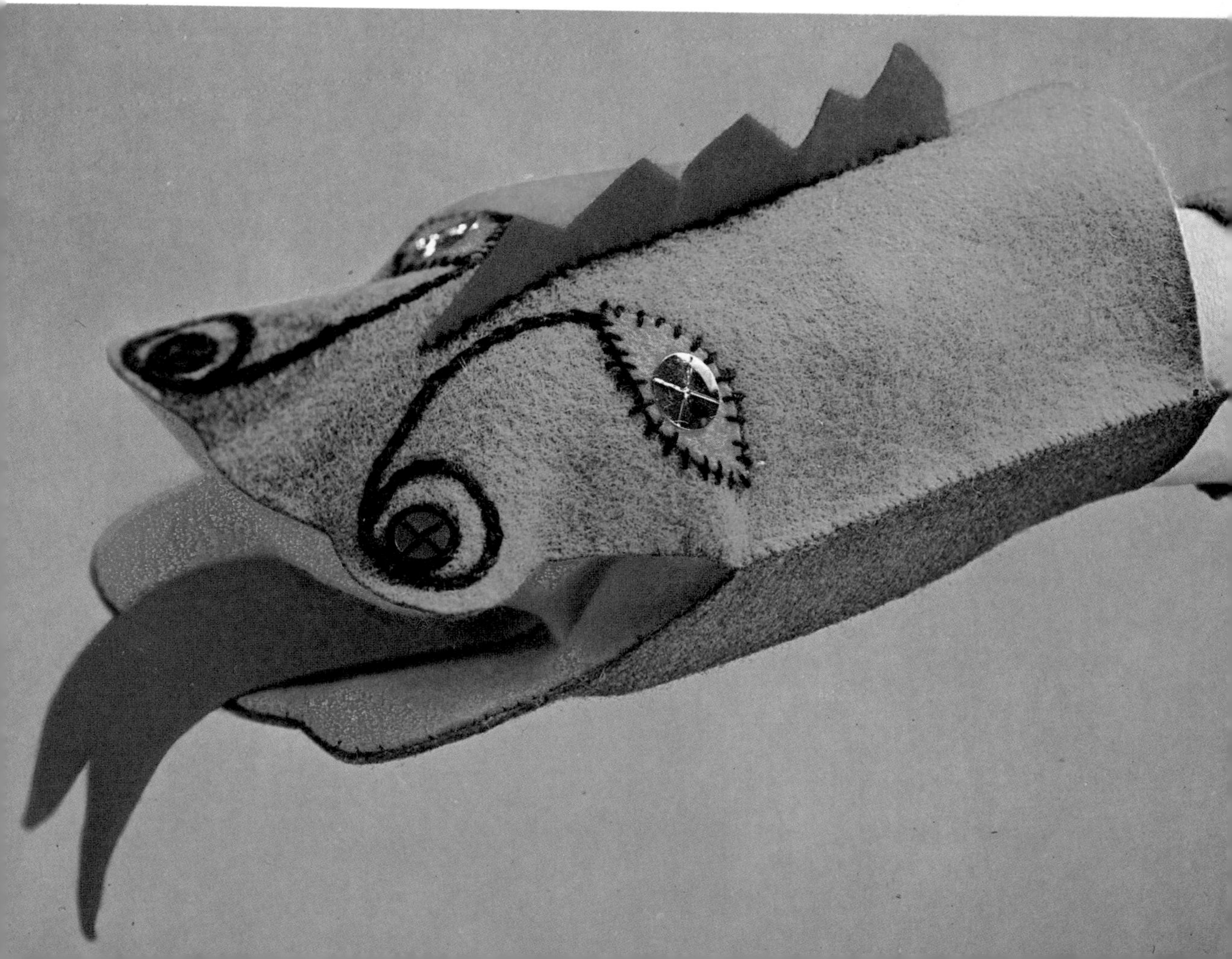

Puppets with arms

The same basic shape of template is used for all the puppets, with simple details added to make the different characters. When adding clothing remember that the front view is important, particularly in a puppet performance before an audience, and this should be kept in mind when 'dressing' the puppet.

When separate faces are added, as in Red Riding Hood, they can be sewn on top of the puppet base, giving extra strength to the head.

When backs of heads are added plus a hat, as in the guardsman, it is better to cut away the under parts of face and back of head or the finished puppet may be top-heavy and badly balanced for small hands to manipulate.

Usually the thumb and little finger are inserted in the puppet's hands and the other three fingers in the head. The facial expression of these puppets cannot be altered by moving the fingers as in the previous puppets.

Smaller children may find a puppet on a stick easier to handle and these puppets can be adapted quite easily to fit on to a piece of dowel rod.

A lion

You will need:

A piece of tawny or orange coloured felt about 25.5 cm by 36 cm (10" by 14"); some scraps of brown felt for features; black embroidery silk; matching cotton; some tawny or light brown wool for the mane; and a template (Fig 29).

Trace the puppet pattern on to a piece of thin card and cut it out. Trace round it on to the piece of felt using a very sharply pointed soft pencil, and cut out two shapes. Keep the pencil-marked side as the wrong side, but if possible, when cutting the shapes, cut just inside the pencil lines, otherwise the finished seam may look grubby.

On one of the pieces arrange the features. Cut a thin oval shape for the nose and sew it on in the middle of the face. Embroider two curving lines from the base

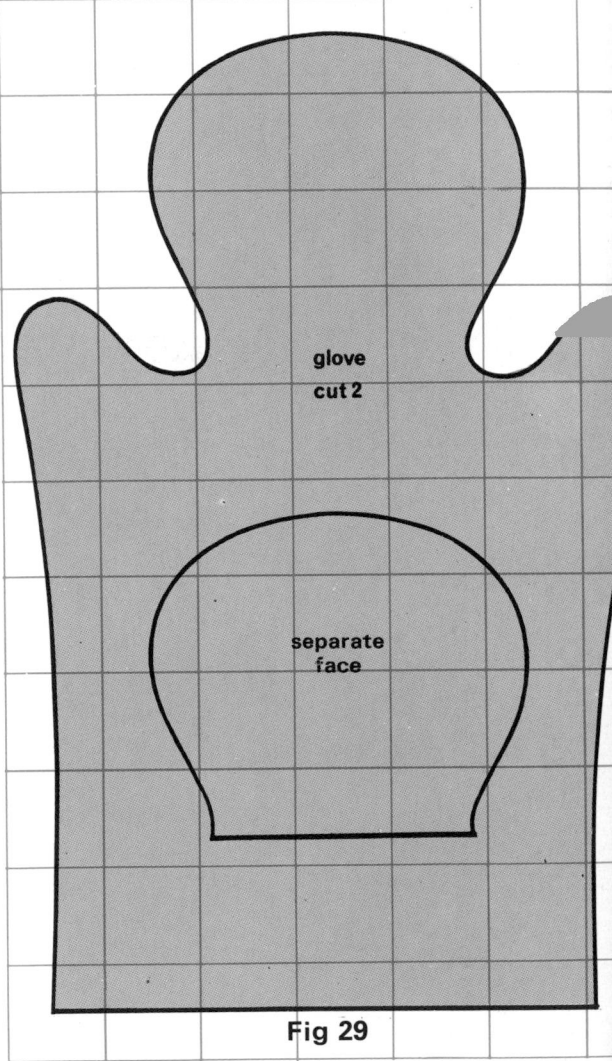

glove
cut 2

separate
face

Fig 29

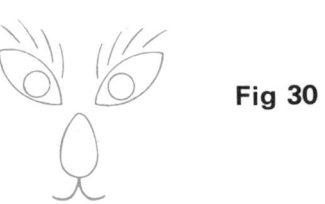

Fig 30

of the nose towards the sides of the face. For the eyes, cut out two ovals pointed at each end, and sew them on at an angle, slanting in towards the nose (Fig 30).

Embroider some long straight stitches along the top edges.

Around the edge, and across the bottom of the face, in a circle work a row of loops close together for the mane, using the wool (Fig 31).

Place the two puppet pieces together with right sides outside, pin them (on the edge of the felt to avoid pin marks) matching the top of the head, hands and bottom edges, and oversew them together with matching cotton. Your lion is ready.

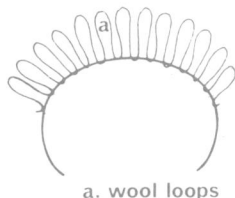

a. wool loops

Fig 31

A policeman

You will need:

Royal blue felt; flesh-coloured felt for the face; brown felt for the back of the head and moustache; black felt for the helmet; red felt for the mouth; silver metal-thread; three small silver beads.

Cut out two puppet shapes in royal blue felt, one face shape in flesh or natural colour and one in brown.

The features

Work on the face first. Cut a crescent shape in red and sew in place for a mouth, and above it a moustache in black or brown felt. Two white ovals with pointed ends and blue circles set in them will do for eyes.

Sew the face piece in place over the royal blue face and cut off the blue one. Repeat this with the back of the head, and sew down at the back also.

Sew three small silver buttons or beads down the front of the tunic.

Cut a strip of blue 9 mm ($\frac{3}{8}$″) wide and long enough to stretch across the front of the neck for a collar. Embroider a small motif in fine silver metal-thread (Fig 32) each side of the centre and sew the band in place over the join of face and tunic.

Sew the two glove pieces together on the right side.

Cut two pieces in black felt from the helmet template (Fig 33). In the centre of one embroider in silver metal-thread a motif similar to, but larger than, the ones on the collar. Oversew the two curved sides of the helmet, fit in place on the head and sew down on the back and front of the head, being careful not to take the stitches through both thicknesses.

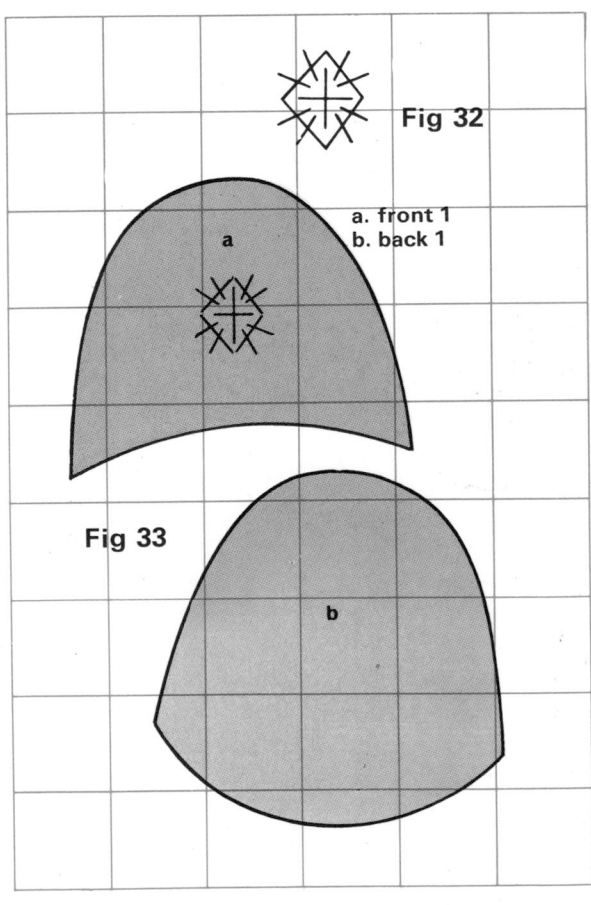

Fig 32

a. front 1
b. back 1

Fig 33

A guardsman

The guardsman glove is cut out in two colours for each piece.

You will need:

Royal blue felt for the lower half for his trousers and scarlet felt for the top for his jacket; natural or flesh-coloured felt for the head and face; black felt for his bearskin and belt; some gold sequins; a little gold metal-thread.

The blue and the red felt each need to measure 23 cm by 9 cm (13″ by 3½″). Place the long edge of blue over the red and tack them together (Fig 34). Lay the template on this so that the bottom edge is level with the edge of the blue felt and the neck is on the edge of the red felt. Cut out two shapes, reversing the template for the second piece.

Place the head part of the template on the flesh-coloured felt, allowing the felt to overlap on to the red for joining, and cut out two head shapes.

The features

Sew the features on to one of the flesh-coloured pieces and then sew the two head pieces together on the right side.

The uniform

Sew the red and blue felt together on both right and wrong sides for strength. Keep stitches from showing through on the right side. On one of the pieces (the front) sew five or six gold sequins in a row for buttons, and embroider a motif in gold thread each side of the centre of the neck.

Trim the neck part of the head pieces to slip inside the red collar and sew it in place with tiny stitches. Sew both pieces together on the right side.

The belt

Cut a strip of black felt about 9 mm (⅜″) wide and long enough to go right round the waist of the glove to hide the join of the red and blue felt. Embroider a buckle shape in gold thread in the centre front of the belt and sew it in place.

The helmet

Cut two helmet pieces in black felt and oversew the two rounded edges (Fig 35). Place in position on the head just over the eyes in front and sew on round the head not allowing the stitches to go through two thicknesses.

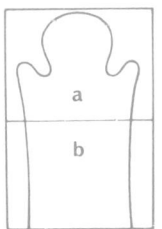

a. red felt
b. blue felt

Fig 34

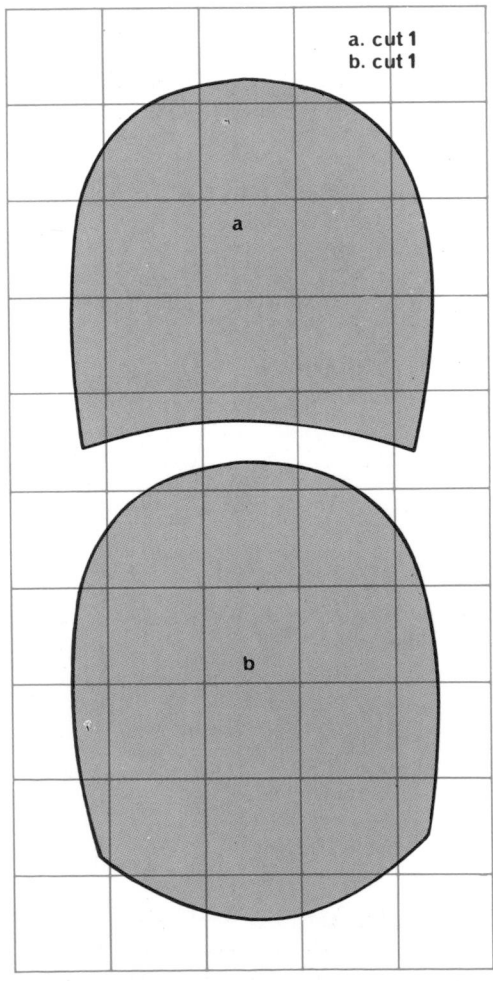

a. cut 1
b. cut 1

Fig 35

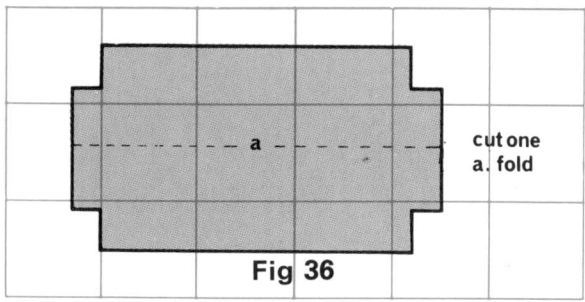

Fig 36

A sailor

You will need:

Royal blue felt; black felt; white felt; a piece of flesh-coloured felt for his face.

Cut out two glove shapes in blue, one head shape in flesh colour and one in black felt. Cut two triangular-shaped pieces in white felt for the front of his collar and a rectangle for the back, curve one side of the rectangle and sew on to the neck of one glove piece. Sew the two triangles on the front piece with the wide ends on the shoulders and the narrow ends meeting at the waist. Finish off with a twist of black felt. Make up the glove in the same way as for the policeman. Cut a narrow, curved piece of white felt long enough to fit along the front of the neck over the join and sew it in place.

The cap

Cut out the cap shape in black felt and fold it in half lengthways (Fig 36). Oversew the two short edges. Across the front sew a narrow strip of white Vilene or felt. Fit it on to the head with a slight slant and sew it in place.

A witch

She is a useful puppet because there is one in nearly every fairy story which can be made into a puppet play.

You will need:

Some black felt; some brownish red for her face; some scraps for features; some grey wool for hair.

Cut out two shapes in black and one face shape in the brownish-red felt.

The features

The eyes are green circles on white; her mouth is a down-turned crescent in red. Pin the face piece to one of the glove pieces and sew them together on the right side. Tease out some grey wool and sew it raggedly on each side of the face.

The hat

Cut about 9 mm ($\frac{3}{8}$") of a 10 cm (4") circle for a hat. Sew together the straight edges, place in position straight over the eyes and sew to the face and head, not letting stitches go through.

A cat puppet on a stick

You will need:

Black felt; a scrap of green felt for eyes; some fine green metal-thread for whiskers; a little stuffing; a piece of dowel rod of the required length.

The cat is cut from the basic pattern with pointed ears added but with the arms omitted and sloping shoulders instead. Before tracing the shape, stick two pointed ears on to the basic template (Fig 37, over page). Cut out two shapes from the felt, reversing the template for the second piece.

Mark the centre of the face and on each side of it embroider some long stitches in fine green metal-thread, for whiskers. Cut two green ovals, pointed at each end, for eyes, and sew on at an angle slanting towards the centre. Add a small circle of black felt for the centre of each eye. Oversew the edges together all round.

Pad the top of the dowel rod with a little wadding and tie it securely (Fig 38). Push it up into the head with more stuffing all round it to keep it in place.

Red Riding Hood – four story puppets

There are four characters in this story, Red Riding Hood the heroine, her grandmother, the wicked wolf and her father, the woodcutter.

Red Riding Hood

You will need:

Pale blue felt for her dress; flesh-coloured felt for her face; red and white felt for her cloak and hood and brown wool for her hair.

Make up the glove, sewing in the face with the glove seams. Cut about eight strands of brown wool 26 cm (10") long and sew

pointed ear

Fig 37

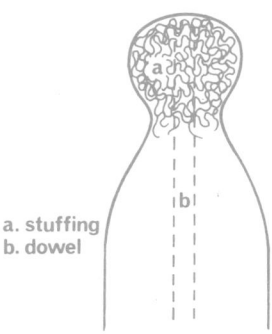

a. stuffing
b. dowel

Fig 38

the middle of them to the top of the head. Embroider a few vertical stitches on the forehead for a fringe. Catch the strands of wool each side of the face and plait the ends.

The hood

Cut a strip of red felt 23 cm by 7 cm (9″ by 2¾″). Fold in half and oversew the edges to make a hood. Fit it round the face so that the front corners fold round on the front of the glove on each side to frame the face. Sew the two front corners to the glove, leaving the back of the hood free.

The cloak

The cloak is a rectangle 14 cm by 11 cm (5½″ by 4½″) the shorter side being sewn on to the back of the hood. Cut two little collar shapes in white Vilene or felt and sew on at the neck to hide the join.

Grannie

You will need:

Purple felt for the dress; grey felt for her face; white wool for hair; lace for her cap.

Grannie's hair

Fig 39

Make her up just like Red Riding Hood. Round her face sew loops of white wool for hair, twist the wool two or three times round a finger, hold the loops close to the face and sew in place (Fig 39). Repeat this, sewing each set of loops as close as possible to the preceding ones. Sew a gathered lace or ribbon frill round her neck and a wider piece of lace over her head for a cap or bonnet.

The wolf

You will need:

Very dark brown, orange, black, red and white felt.

The wolf's eyes are orange with black centres, sewn on at an angle slanting in to the centre of the face.

The snout is sewn on in two parts, an upper and a lower, so that it juts from the face with its red tongue hanging out at one side.

The mouth

The red lining to the mouth is cut in shape like a pointed ear (Fig 40) with the sides curving from a straight base to a point. The white interlining and the brown outer

Wolf's snout

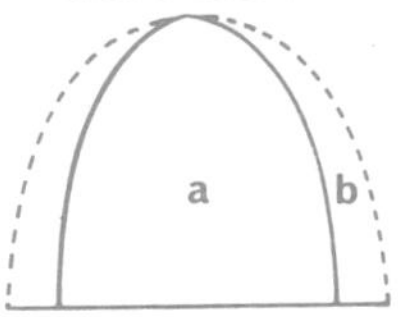

a. red felt lining
b. Vilene and brown felt

Fig 40

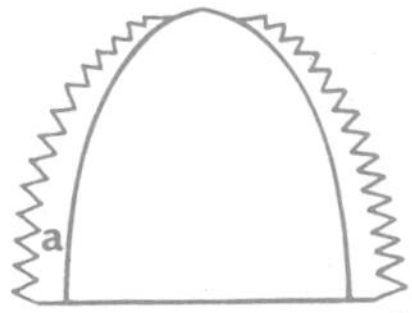

a. white Vilene notched

Fig 41

a. brown felt
b. face
c. red lining

Fig 42

cover are similar in shape to the red but curve from a much wider base (Fig 41).

Cut two brown pieces, two red pieces and two white interlining pieces. Sew the red piece on to the white interlining in the middle so that an edge of white stands out all round the curved sides of the red. Cut the protruding white edge into notches, for teeth (Fig 41). Place the brown felt shape on top of the white so that its curved edges are sewn on to those of the red felt. Because the straight edge of the brown piece is longer than the straight edge of the red it will be like an arch over the red (Fig 42). Sew it with ladder stitch on to the face following the curve of the brown felt (Fig 40).

The tongue

Make up the other part of the mouth to match but before sewing it on to the face, cut a long tongue shape in red felt and sew the narrower end of it on to the straight edge of the red felt (the back of the throat) so that it hangs out to one side. Sew the part on to the face so that the two red linings are set close together and the two brown edges form a circle.

Ears

The ears are curved leaf shapes — cut four of them and sew two outer curves of each together for each ear. Cut the other edges into feather-shaped notches. Pin them in place on the head and sew them in with the seam as you sew the two glove pieces together.

The woodcutter, father of Red Riding Hood

You will need:

Dark green felt; flesh-coloured felt; brown felt; red felt; white felt.

Cut the glove in dark green felt with the face in flesh colour and the back of the head in brown felt. He has a curved crescent of red for a mouth with a moustache in brown felt above it. Two brown circles on white pointed ovals are his eyes. His beard is a triangle of brown felt with one curving side and the pointed end cut into a fringe and sewn on under

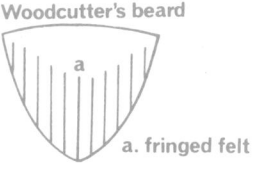
Woodcutter's beard

a. fringed felt

Fig 43

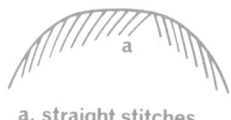
a. straight stitches

Fig 44

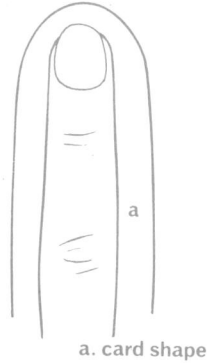
a. card shape

Fig 45

the mouth (Fig 43). All these features are sewn on to the flesh-coloured face.

Sew the face piece on to one glove and the brown head on to the other at the neck edge, afterwards cutting away the green head from the glove. Sew the glove pieces together. Hair is made by sewing slanting stitches on the top edge of the face (Fig 44).

Many more characters can be made from these puppet templates, and characters from any traditional or original stories or rhymes will turn them into realistic plays.

Finger puppets

These are very small characters and because of this must be kept very simple and not in the least fussy. All kinds of small pieces of felt can be used because the back and front need not necessarily be the same colour. They are just big enough to fit over a finger for half its length, to the middle knuckle.

The template for them is easily made by placing a finger flat on a piece of card and drawing round it leaving a 6 mm ($\frac{1}{4}$") margin of extra width all round (Fig 45). (If the longest finger is used you will be sure that the finished puppet will fit any other finger.) Use this template to trace round on the felt and cut out two pieces for each puppet.

A girl

You will need:

Pale pink felt; some yellow silk or floss or wool for hair; pink embroidery silk; blue embroidery silk; some beads.

Cut two pieces in pink felt. Sew the mouth first — one long and one short stitch each side of the centre in pink embroidery silk (Fig 46). The eyes are two open-ended single chain stitches with blue spots in the corners and straight stitch eyelashes (Fig 47). Sew some straight stitches in yellow down the forehead for a fringe (Fig 48). Cut short lengths of yellow silk, sew in the middle on top of the head and bring the ends down each side of the face.

For a necklace start off with sewing cotton at one side of the neck, thread on sufficient beads to make a short loop and fasten off at the other side.

Sew the two felt pieces together on the right side.

Fig 46   **Fig 47**

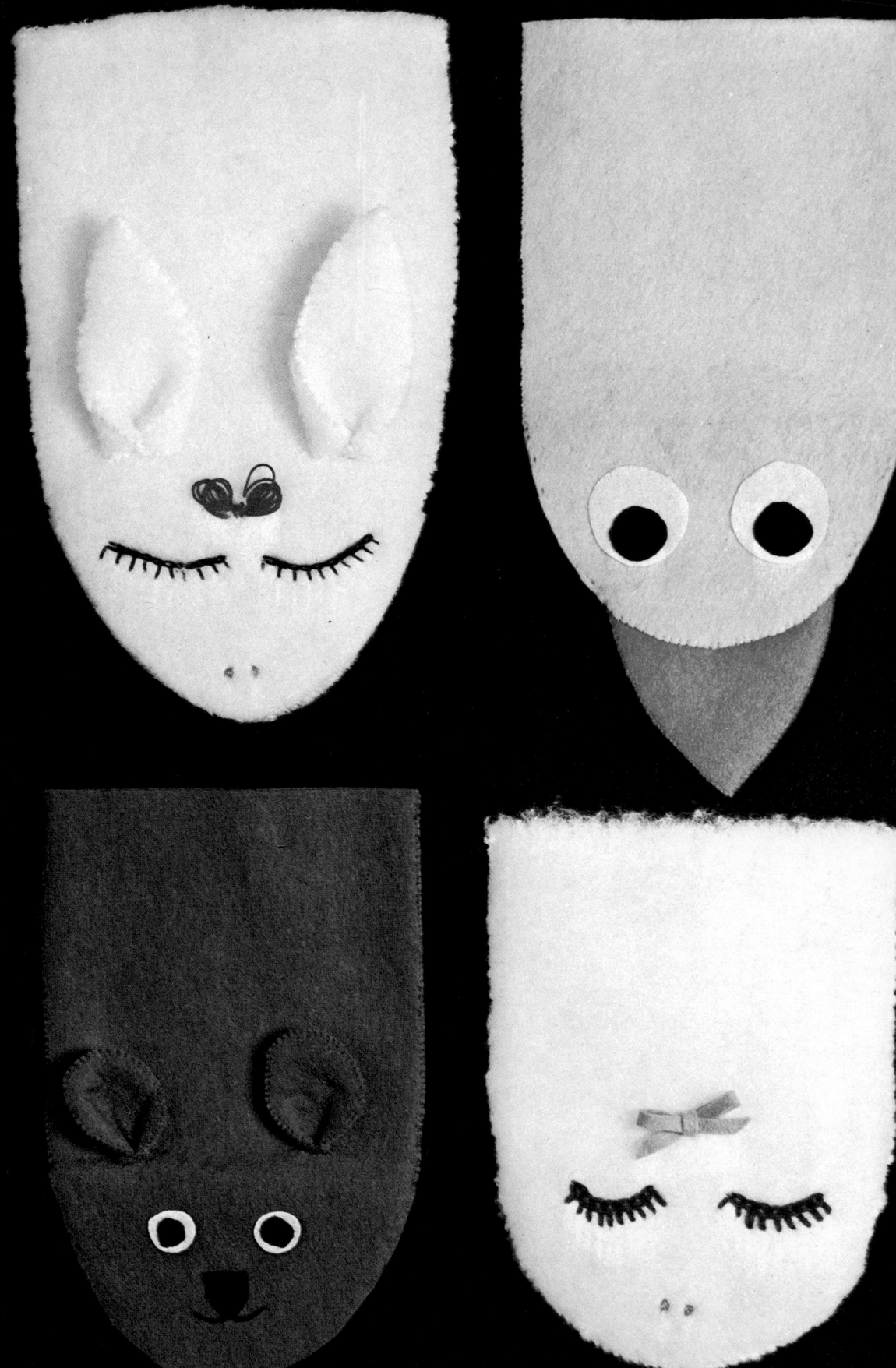

Fig 48

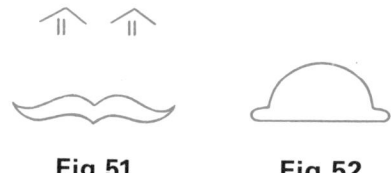

Fig 51   **Fig 52**

A lion

You will need:

Orange, beige felt; tawny wool; embroidery silk.

Cut two pieces in orange felt. A thin oval in beige or brown felt is sewn down the middle of the face for a nose and the mouth is two curved lines embroidered in stem stitch from the bottom of the nose. Eyes are two single chain stitches slanting in to the nose with a centre spot. Sew loops of tawny wool all round the face for a mane and sew the two felt pieces together (Fig 49).

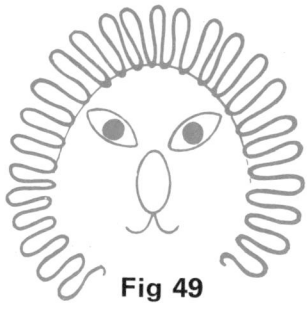

Fig 49

A man

You will need:

Pink, black, red and white felt; embroidery silk.

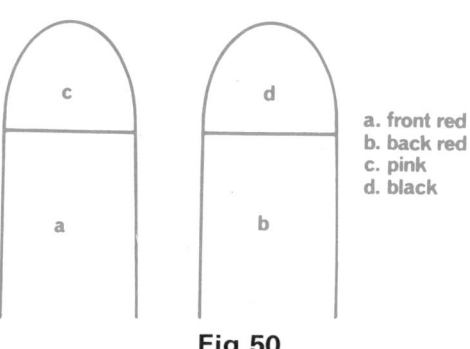

a. front red
b. back red
c. pink
d. black

Fig 50

The front and back are treated differently. The curved end is cut in pink for the face and black for the back of the head (Fig 50) and both joined on to red felt to make each piece the right size. Embroider the mouth as you did for the girl. The eyes are two small straight stitches with two straight stitches over them at an angle (Fig 51). The moustache can be cut in black felt and sewn on in the middle leaving the ends free, or it can be embroidered.

Sew the two pieces together, matching the felts. Cut a small collar in white and sew on over the join. The hat is in black felt, sewn on across the head (Fig 52).

A rabbit

This can be made in white felt or man-made fibre. The ears are lined with pink felt. Cut two shapes in white. Cut two white ears and two pink ears. Embroider a round pink spot for a nose with three or four whiskers each side. Sew together one pink felt piece and one white piece for each ear. Fold the corners in to the middle and sew on to the face piece with the pink sides forward. Sew the back and front together on the right sides (Fig 53).

Fig 53

CHAPTER FOUR

Toys from shapes

circles, ovals and rectangles

If you doodle when you are thinking, you will know how the doodles take all kinds of fantastic and imaginative shapes. Some of the toys here are like that because they can be evolved from many different shapes — circles, squares, ovals — placed together in various ways, to achieve a shape, or something recognizable.

A cat from circles

You will need:

Felt; embroidery silks; kapok; cotton for sewing; ribbon; card.

Draw a 15 cm (6") circle for the body with a 10 cm (4") circle above it and over-lapping it to form a head and neck.

On the smaller circle draw two triangles with curved sides for ears, and extend the curve at the base of the large circle to make a curled tail (Fig 1). This shape when cut out will be your template.

Trace round it twice, reversing the template the second time to keep the pencil marks all on the one side (Fig 2).

Oversew the two pieces together, leaving an opening at the base. Fill it smoothly with small pieces of kapok, pushing it gently into the corners of ears and tail, not too hard — it should be flat rather than fat.

Sew up the opening.

Cut a shield shape in black felt for a nose, and sew in position.

Embroider two curves for the mouth in

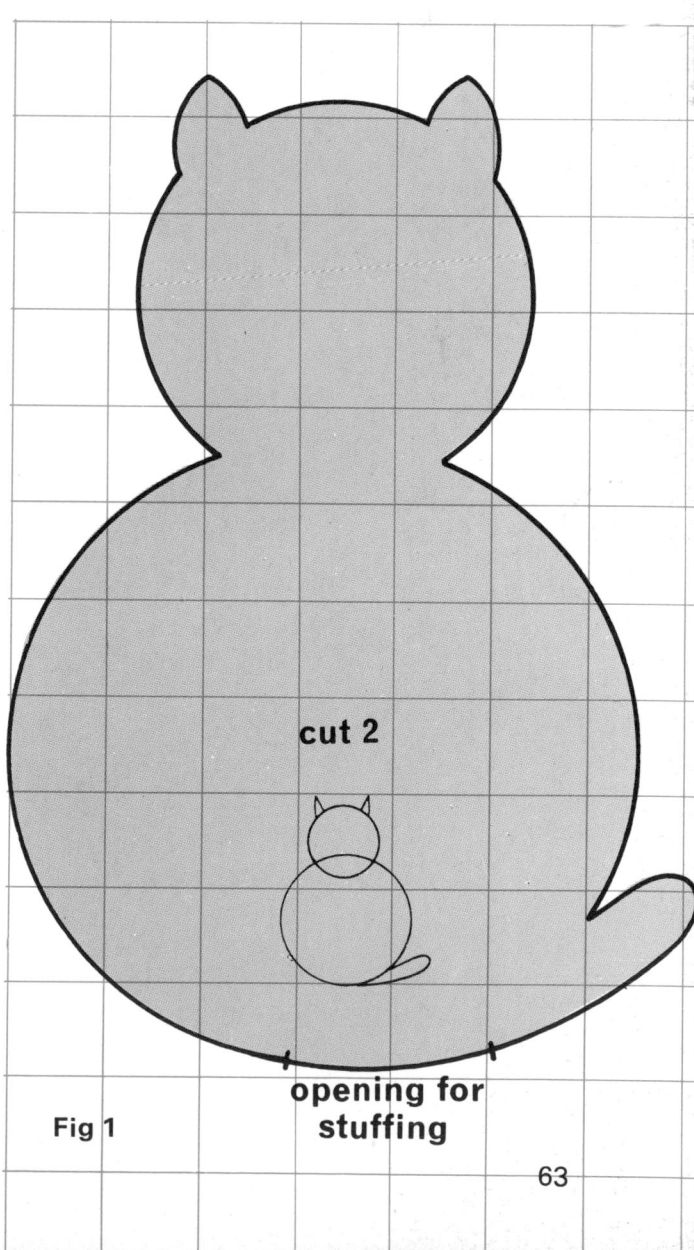

cut 2

opening for
stuffing

Fig 1

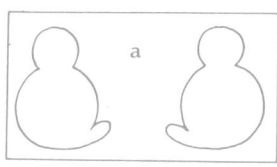

a. felt

Fig 2

Fig 3

stem or chain stitch and straight stitches in black silk for whiskers (Fig 3).

Cut two ovals with pointed ends, and two black centres, for eyes, and sew them in position on the face, slanting in towards the nose. Tie a bright ribbon or felt bow round its neck.

A little blue bird

You will need:

Blue felt; pink felt for the wings; scraps of orange and white felt for the eyes, beak and feet; thin card; embroidery silks; sewing cotton; kapok.

Draw a 15 cm (6") circle on the card, and add a triangle to it at one side to form a pointed tail (Fig 4). Draw a gusset shape, pointed at each end, 5 cm (2") wide in the middle and long enough to stretch from under the beak to the tail. In a triangle 9 cm by 4 cm (3½" by 1½") draw the wing shape, and the feet in a diamond 4 cm by 2.5 cm (1½" by 1") (Fig 5). The beak is a curved triangle.

Cut two body pieces and one gusset in blue felt, two wing shapes in pink, four feet, two beaks and two eyes in orange, two slightly larger black circles and two much larger white circles, also for the eyes.

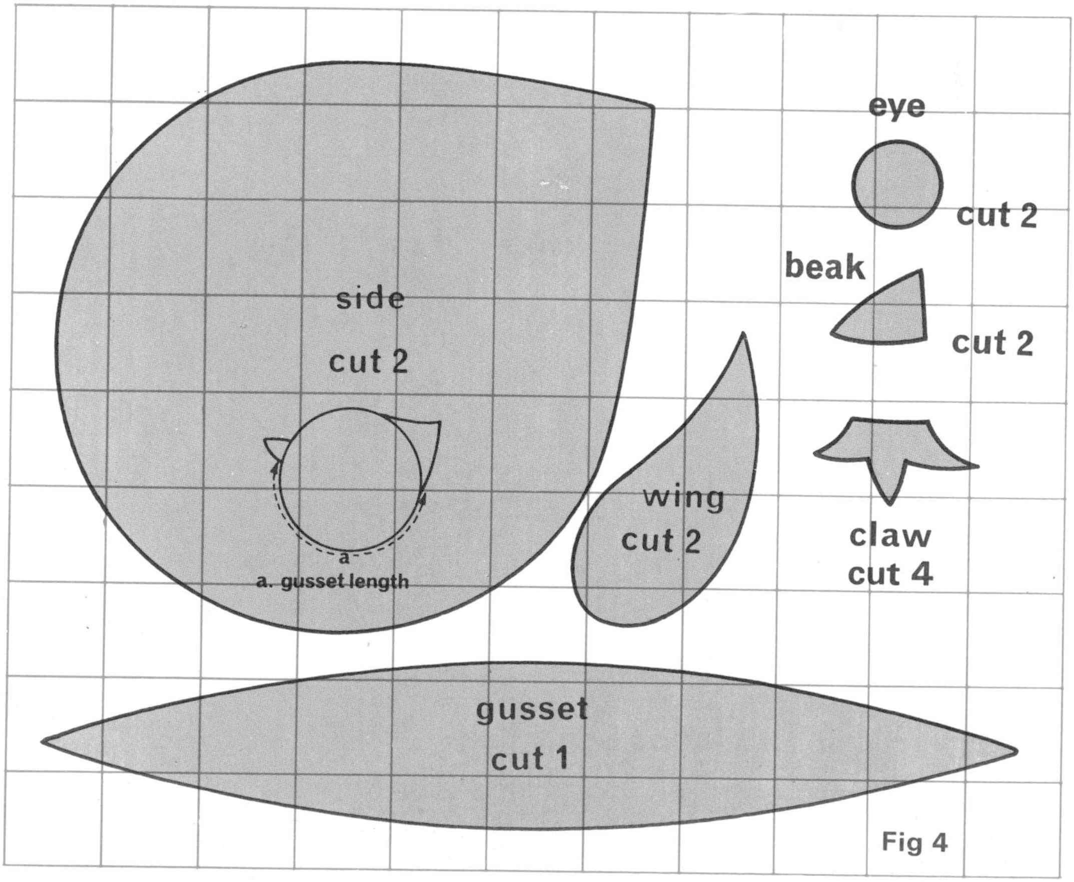

side

cut 2

a. gusset length

eye

cut 2

beak

cut 2

wing

cut 2

claw

cut 4

gusset

cut 1

Fig 4

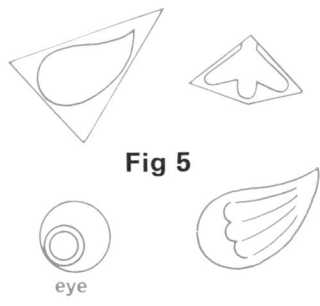

Fig 5

eye

Fig 6

Embroider the wings in a feather design, pairing them for left and right (Fig 6).

Sew two shapes together for each foot and sew the two beak shapes together.

Place a black circle under an orange one so that it shows a rim of black and sew both of them near to one edge of a white circle. Sew them together (Fig 6).

Sew wings, eyes and feet in position on each side piece, matching the positions of each one.

Sew the gusset to one side piece, starting at the tail. Pin it to the second side at matching points and sew it, leaving an opening at the tail for the filling. Pin the beak in position where the gusset joins the side, and sew it. Oversew the top edges of the bird.

Fill it smoothly, not too hard, with small pieces of kapok. Sew up the opening.

A rabbit from ovals

You will need:

Felt; kapok; card; sewing cotton.

Draw a large and a small oval overlapping at the ends. Add a smaller oval at the opposite end of the large oval for a tail, add two long oval ears, and an oval front paw (Fig 7).

Cut out this shape in the card and trace round it on to the piece of felt.

Cut two shapes in felt, reversing the template for the second one, pin them together with the pencilled sides inside and sew them together, leaving an opening in the base.

Push small pieces of kapok carefully into ears, tail and front paw. Stuff the head, then the rest of the body. Sew up the opening. Work a nose and mouth in single chain stitch (Fig 8) and three or four straight stitches each side for whiskers.

eye

nose

a

a. single chain stitch

Fig 8

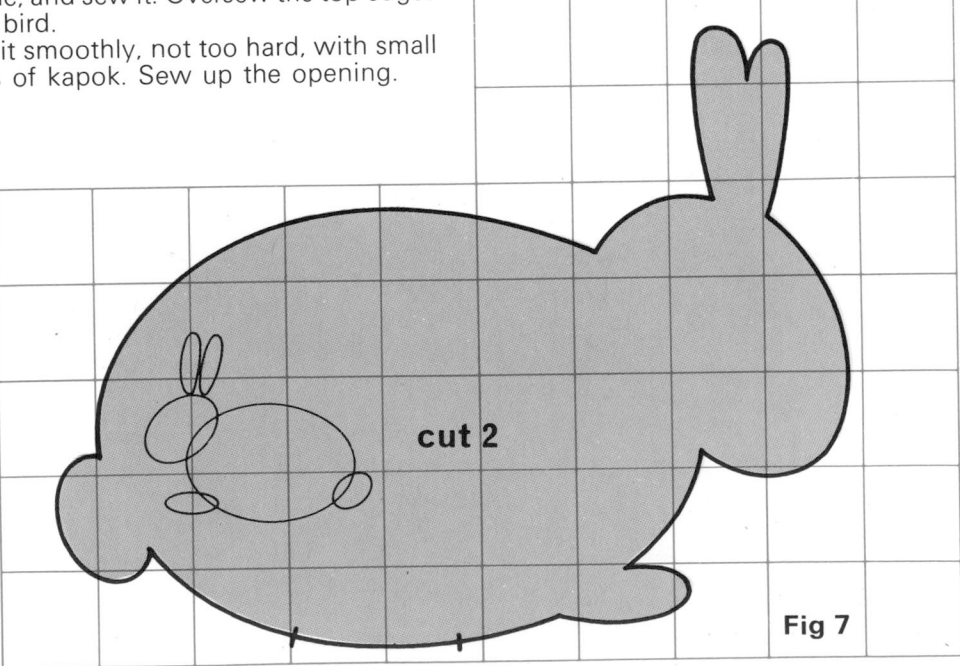

cut 2

Fig 7

A giraffe

He is made from a circle, a rectangle and a triangle (Fig 9).

You will need:
A piece of blue felt; scraps of orange felt for ears; black felt for the mane and tail; some kapok; orange embroidery silk; cotton; thin card.

Draw a 15 cm (6") circle and a 9 cm (3½") circle inside it from the same centre. Draw a line across the circle 4 cm (1½") from the edge.

Cut off this piece and cut out the centre circle (Fig 10). This shape is for the giraffe's legs and body.

From the point X on the circle (Fig 10a) draw a rectangle 12.5 cm (5") long and 2.5 cm (1") wide. Draw a triangle at the top of this neck for a head (Fig 10b).

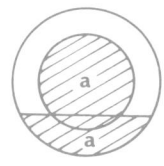

a. cut away

Fig 10

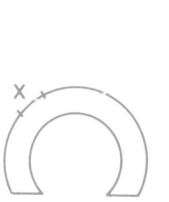

Fig 10a

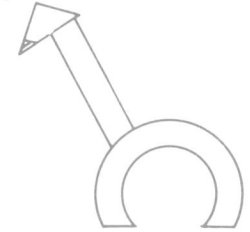

Fig 10b

cut 2

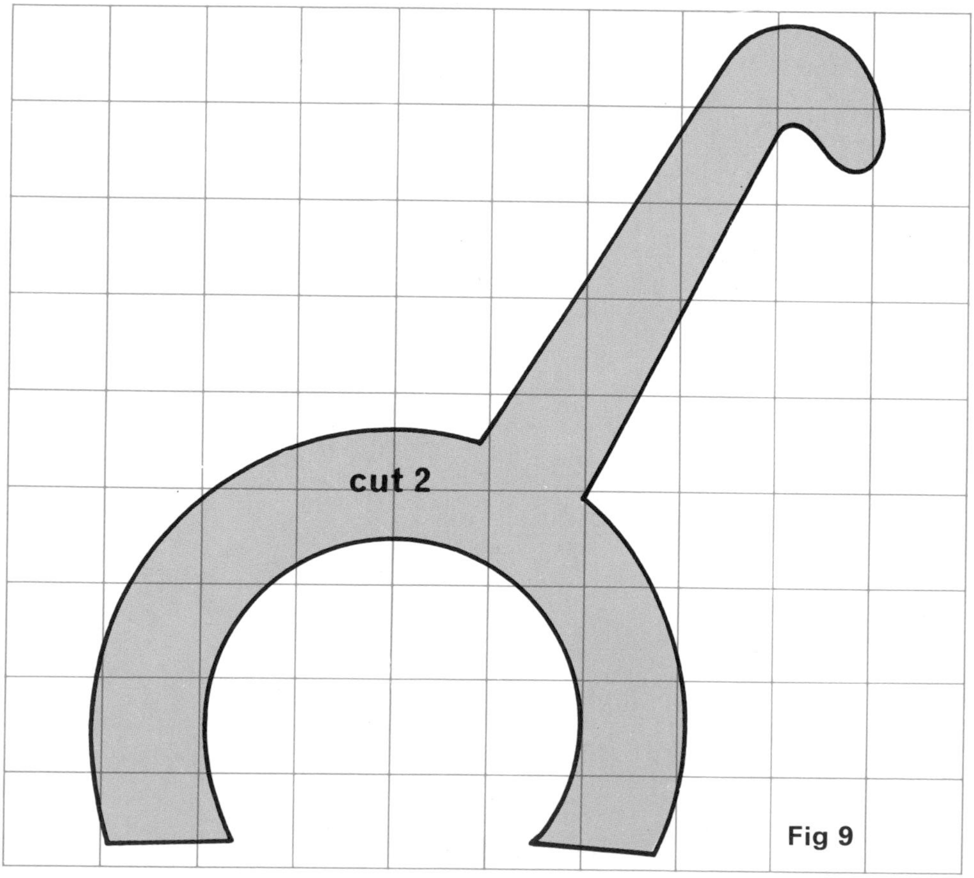

Fig 9

Round off the corners at the top of the head and the mouth. This figure forms the template.

Cut out two pieces in blue felt. Cut a narrow strip of black felt for a mane and two triangular pieces for a tail. Cut two small rectangles of black for horns and two ears in orange felt.

Pin the mane on to one side piece from the top of the head to halfway down the neck. Pin the two tail pieces in position. Pin the two body pieces together.

Oversew together the inner edges of the circle. Sew the base and the outer edge of the front leg as far as the neck. Lightly fill the front leg with kapok. Oversew the front edges of the neck and over the head. Stuff the head.

Continue sewing down the back of the neck, sewing in the mane at the same time and filling with kapok as you work. Sew the body and the back leg, sewing in the tail as well, still filling with kapok.

Roll up two small rectangles of felt and stitch them to form horns. Sew them in place on top of the head with ladder stitch, taking a stitch first in the head, then in the horn. Fold the bases of the ears in half and sew them in place slightly below and behind the horns.

Embroider the eyes and mouth.

A snake from cylinders

The snake's head and tail are cone-shaped and each segment is a cylinder. For this one (Fig 11), with six segments, head and tail:

You will need:

A piece of felt 6.5 cm by 13 cm ($2\frac{1}{2}$″ by $5\frac{1}{4}$″) and two circles 4.5 cm ($1\frac{3}{4}$″) diameter (the head is 10 cm (4″) long, pointed at one end and a 4.5 cm ($1\frac{3}{4}$″) circle at the other — the tail is 15 cm (6″) long, shaped like the head); some bright embroidery silks; some kapok; matching cotton for sewing; sequins or scraps of felt for eyes and tongue; tinsel cord for threading.

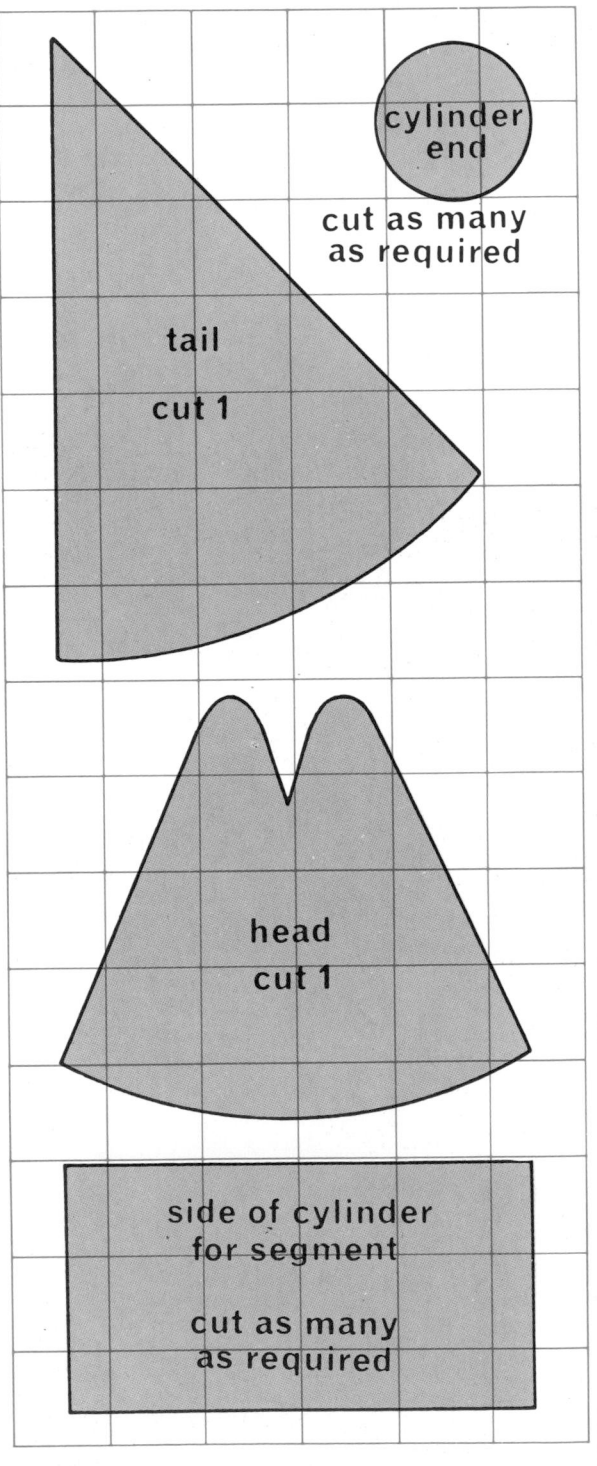

cylinder end

cut as many as required

tail

cut 1

head

cut 1

side of cylinder for segment

cut as many as required

Fig 11

fly stitch

Fig 12

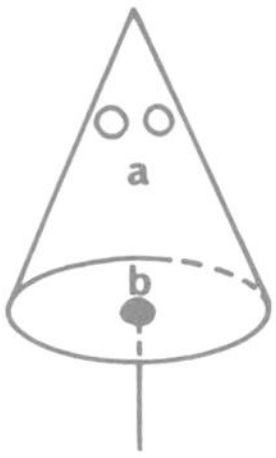

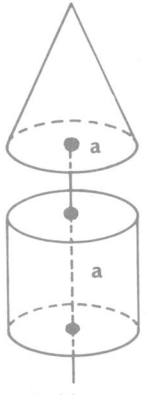

a. head
b. knot inside

Fig 13

a. inside

Fig 14

Sew the eyes and tongue in position on the head and embroider a design in fly stitch down the back (Fig 12), in the middle. Oversew the side seams.

Make a small hole in the centre of the circle, thread in the cord and knot it securely (Fig 13). Push kapok gently into the pointed end of the head.

Pin on the circle and oversew the edges, pushing in any extra stuffing if needed.

Embroider a fly-stitch design down the centre of the cylinder piece and sew the side seam.

Thread an end of cord through one circle and knot it securely to hold it in place. Thread the end through the felt tube, and sew a circle on to it. Make a second knot to come just inside the tube, stuff round the cord, thread the cord through the second circle and sew the circle on to complete the cylinder. The knots inside each end of the cylinder will hold it in place on the cord (Fig 14). Continue in the same way with each remaining cylinder.

For the tail, knot the cord inside the circle, thread the cord right through the tail and make a knot outside. Cut a short length of cord, knot it at each end and sew it in the tail so that the three ends form an extension of the felt tail.

Embroider a fly-stitch design over each side seam of the cylinders and of the head and tail.

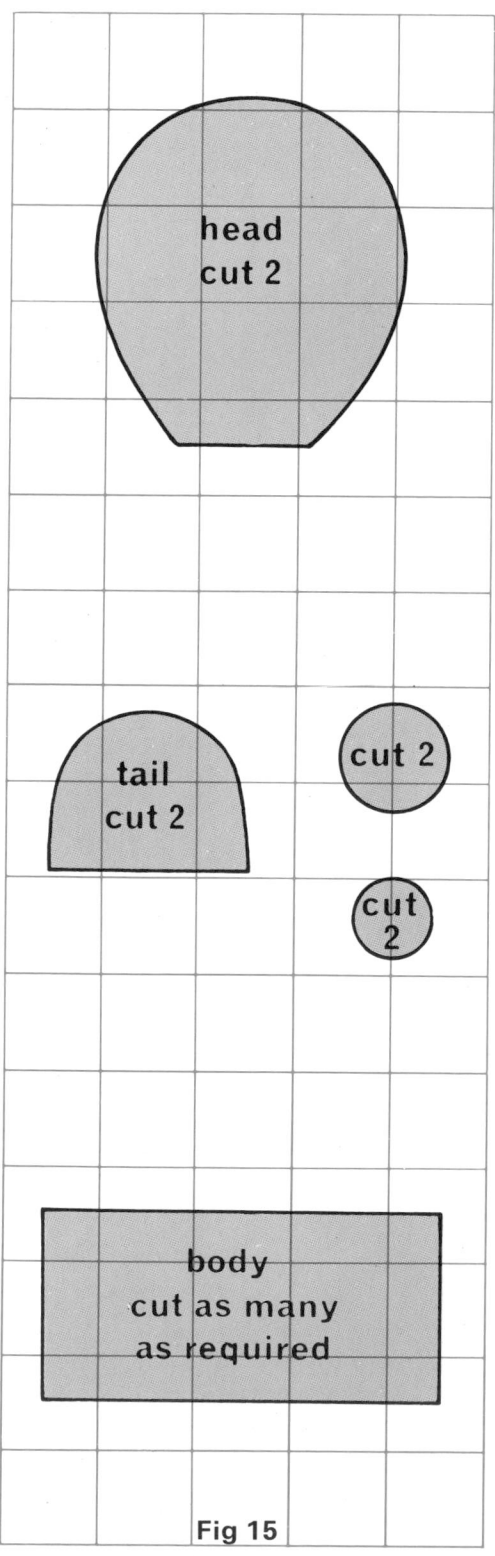

Fig 15

A caterpillar

He is made of rectangles which are folded to form squares, in bright shades of orange, yellow and green felt. His head is an oval, straight-edged at one end, and the tail is an extended semi-circle. He is in twelve segments, but you can make him longer or shorter as you wish (Fig 15).

You will need:

Ten rectangles of felt measuring 10 cm by 5 cm (4" by 2"); two semi-circles on a 5 cm (2") diameter, and extended to measure 5 cm (2") from the outside edge of the curve to the diameter (Fig 16); two ovals measuring 10 cm by 7.5 cm (4" by 3") for the eyes; two large black circles; two white ones half the size and two yellow ones slightly smaller than the white ones; and a 2 cm ($\frac{3}{4}$") wide strip of black felt 60 cm (24") long (this could be in pieces joined, with the joins hidden in the segments); kapok for stuffing; embroidery silks. (Alternatively, to use up smaller pieces of felt, you could have twenty squares sewn together in twos to make the ten segments.)

Cut a piece off the ends of the head ovals to make a straight edge. Sew them together round the curved edges and push in some stuffing (not too much, keeping it flat rather than round).

Sew the straight ends together, enclosing one end of the black strip. Fold a rectangle in half and oversew the two short sides together. Fold it so that the seam is in the middle at the back and thread it on to the black strip. Oversew the edges, enclosing the black strip as well, leaving about 3 mm ($\frac{1}{8}$") to 6 mm ($\frac{1}{4}$") between it and the head (Fig 17). Push in some stuffing and sew up the second side, again sewing in the black strip.

Continue like this with the rest of the rectangles, taking care to keep all the seams on the same side. Sew together the curved sides of the tail pieces and, after stuffing, sew the black strip in with the straight sides of it. There should be the same width of strip left between each segment.

Place a yellow circle on a white oval, slightly to one side, and sew both on to a black circle to one side of it (Fig 18). Sew them in position on the head.

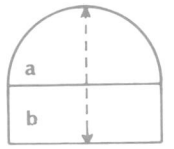

a. semi circle 5 cm
   (2") diameter
b. extension

Fig 16

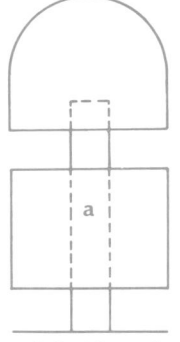

a. felt strip enclosed

Fig 17

eye

Fig 18

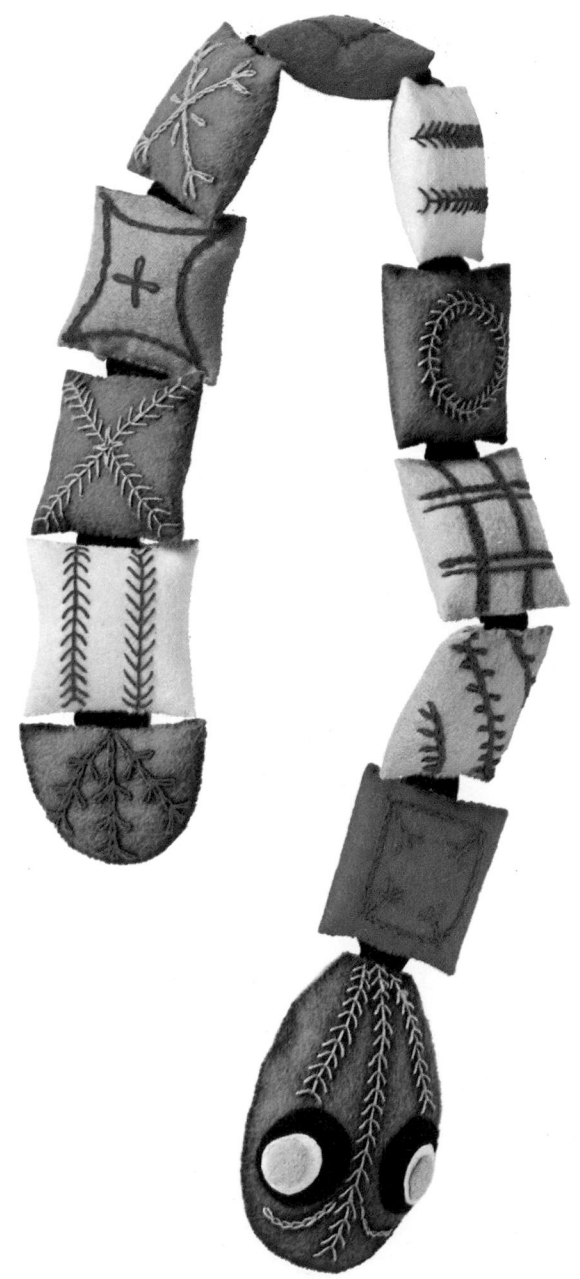

Embroider a line of contrasting fly stitch down the centre of the head, a line pointing to each eye and curls of chain stitch in front. Embroider each segment in a different design in contrasting embroidery silks.

1. A square of chain stitch with a chain stitch flower in each corner.

2. A diagonal of chain stitch with a line each side of it and single chain stitches at the sides.

3. A plaid design in stem stitch, chain and herringbone stitch.

4. A circle of fly stitch.

5. Parallel lines of fly stitch.

6. A diamond of threaded running stitch with the centre of four fly stitches.

7. Diagonal cross of chain stitch with single chain stitches on the ends and in the centre.

8. Curved square of chain stitch with a single chain-stitch centre.

9. Diagonal cross of fly stitch, worked from each corner.

10. Parallel lines of fly stitch.

Tail – three lines of chain stitch spraying out from the straight edges with single chain stitches at the ends and down the sides.

CHAPTER FIVE

Two-piece toys

These toys are made from two pieces of material: two shapes sewn together and filled either with soft stuffing like kapok or foam chippings for a soft cuddly toy, or partly filled with rice or lentils for a slithery toy which can be used for throwing like a ball – it is much easier to catch because it is not a hard shape – or for sliding across a shiny surface.

Any fairly solid-looking round or square shape is suitable. The slither toy, whether it is a round, fat bird, a sitting cat, a duck, frog, fish or tortoise, should be unfussy with no hanging bits and pieces and only soft embroidery.

A slither tortoise

You will need:

A piece of felt about 30 cm by 23 cm (12" by 9") to make a toy 20 cm (8") long, or two pieces in different colours for top and bottom (choose a fairly dark colour for the underside, or any strong cotton material); a card template; embroidery silks; sewing cotton; rice or lentils.

Draw an oval of the size you want your tortoise to be and add a blunt head, a pointed tail and four short legs (Fig 1).

Trace round this on to the felt or material. If you choose felt, cut round the pencil line, but if cotton material is used, cut round 1 cm ($\frac{1}{2}$") outside the line to allow for turnings.

Draw a wavy line all round, just inside the edge of the piece. This will be the top of the tortoise (Fig 2). Criss-cross inside it with wavy lines to indicate the pattern on the shell. Embroider on the lines and round the edge in stem stitch or whipped running stitch.

Place the pieces together with the right sides outside and pin them together at the head, tail and legs. Oversew the edges with

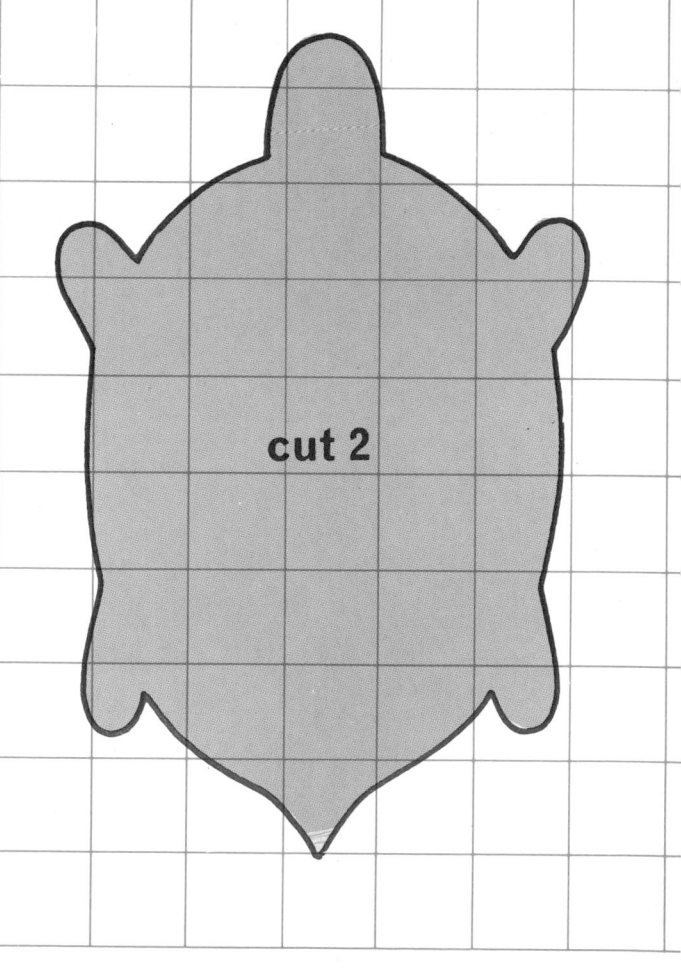

cut 2

Fig 1

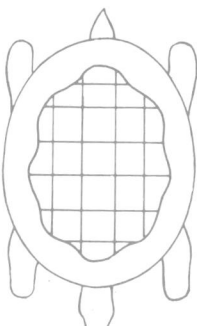

Fig 2

matching cotton, leaving the tail end open.

Pour in spoonfuls of rice until it is about a third or less full — if you have made a large size then pour in less than this proportion, or the finished toy will be much too heavy. Sew up the opening.

If you are using cotton material, embroider the top piece on the side which is not pencilled, taking care to keep the pattern inside the allowance for turnings. Pin the two pieces together at head, tail and legs with right side inside. Machine or backstitch all round the pencil line, leaving the tail end open. Trim off some of the turning allowance, cut out little 'v's on the curves to allow the seams to lie flat and not pucker. Turn it inside out and press the seams flat.

Pour in the filling, turn in the seam allowance at the tail-end opening and sew together either with ladder stitch or oversewing.

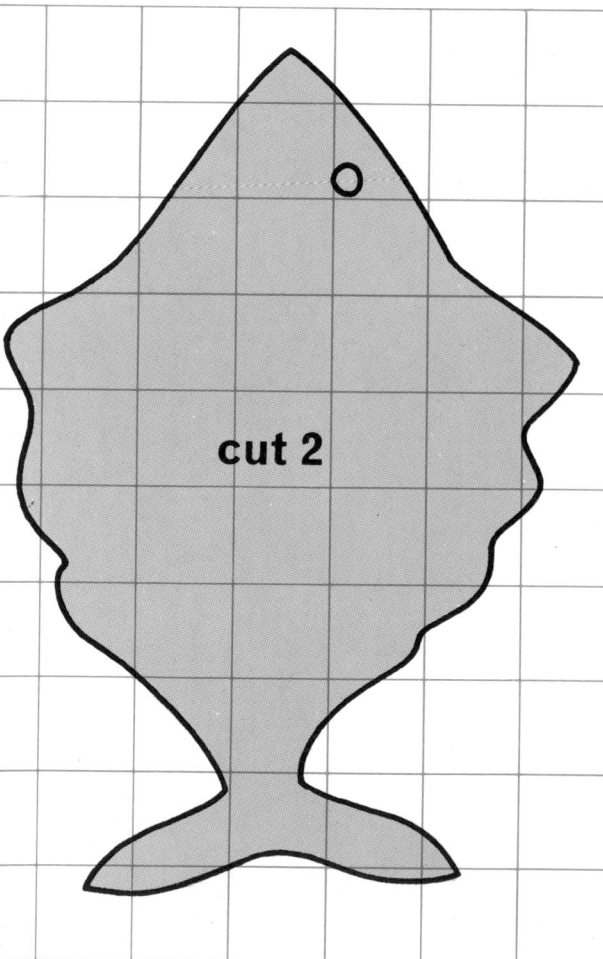

cut 2

Fig 3

A slither fish

You will need:

A piece of felt 30 cm by 24 cm (12" by 9½") to make a 23 cm (9") fish, or two pieces of different colour each measuring 15 cm by 24 cm (6" by 9½"); some rice or lentils for filling; some embroidery silks; matching sewing cotton.

Trace round the template (Fig 3) on the felt and cut out two pieces. If using material not felt be careful to leave about 1 cm (½") allowance for turnings. This will not be so easy to sew at the tail because of the narrow base, so use felt if possible.

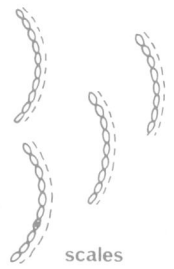

scales

Fig 4

eye

Fig 5

On the piece for the top embroider little crescents in chain stitch to resemble scales and a wavy line all round from the head, along the base of the fins and the base of the tail (Fig 4). Sew on a circle of white felt, or embroider a big eye (Fig 5). Pin the two sides together with right sides outside and pin at the mouth, fins and tail. Oversew the edges all round, leaving the tail end open for stuffing. Pour in rice or chosen filling, not more than a third full, and oversew the tail edges. Sew right through the base of the tail so that no rice can get into it.

A slither frog

You will need:

A piece of felt 26 cm by 48 cm (10$\frac{1}{2}$" by 19") to make a 25 cm (10") frog, or two pieces 26 cm by 24 cm (10$\frac{1}{2}$" by 9$\frac{1}{2}$"); rice for filling; embroidery silks.

Cut out two pieces from the template (Fig 6) and embroider one piece for the top with big eyes, or sew on circles of felt, and some coloured spots on his back. Oversew all round on the right sides, leaving the tail open. Sew across the base of each leg to prevent the filling getting in, because the weight of it can weaken the felt across the narrow base and in the toes. Fill to much less than a third and sew up the opening.

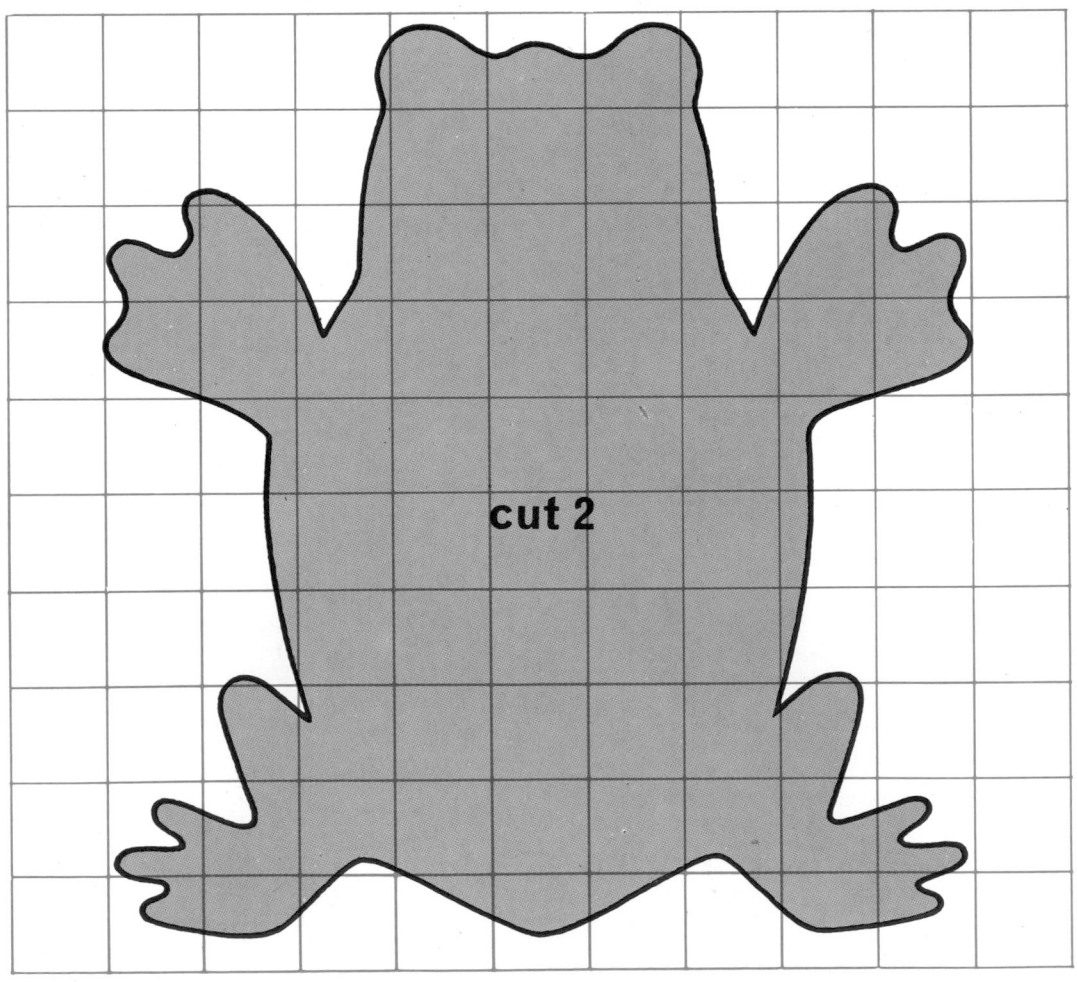

cut 2

Fig 6

Softly stuffed two-piece toys

Because these are flat toys they should not have too much stuffing; otherwise the stitches will pull tight and the seams will pucker and maybe split. Any fairly simple shape makes a satisfactory toy.

A dog

You will need:

Felt; stuffing; embroidery silks; sewing cotton.

Cut out two pieces from your pattern or template drawing, reversing the template to trace the second side so that all pencil markings will be on the wrong side, and embroider an eye on each piece. Template Fig 7.

Pin the pieces together with right sides outside, at nose, ears, tail and feet. Oversew the edges, starting at the inner edge of the front leg and sewing round it (Fig 8), and on over the head to the back of the neck. Stop here and stuff the head and front leg with small pieces of stuffing, pushing it gently into the corners and seams of the foot and head. Continue sewing over the back and the back leg. Sew half of the inner leg seam and then stuff the back foot. Sew the rest of the leg, stuff it and stuff the body. Sew up the under-body seam. Be very careful not to stuff too hard.

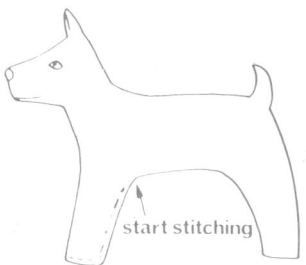

start stitching

Fig 8

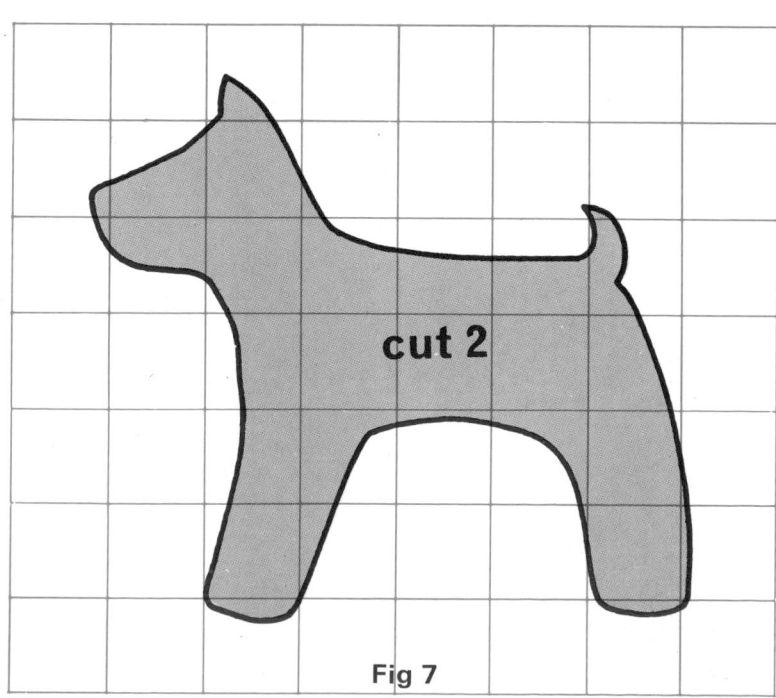

cut 2

Fig 7

A sitting cat

The template is in one piece with ears and tail included, similar to the cat drawn from circles in Chapter Four. This one has a more natural shape.

You will need:

A piece of felt 26 cm by 30 cm ($10\frac{1}{2}$" by 12") to make a 25 cm (10") cat; small piece of green felt for eyes; some stuffing; some embroidery silks; matching cotton.

Cut out two shapes from the template and pin the pieces together, matching ears, neck, and tail (Fig 9).

Oversew the edges, beginning at the base of the tail; stuff the tail when it is sewn and then continue sewing until the head is finished. Stuff the head and continue sewing, leaving the bottom edge open. Stuff the cat's body, keeping it smooth and soft. Sew up the opening.

Embroider green eyes or sew on ovals of green felt, slanting slightly inwards, a black nose and whiskers. Tie a bow round her neck.

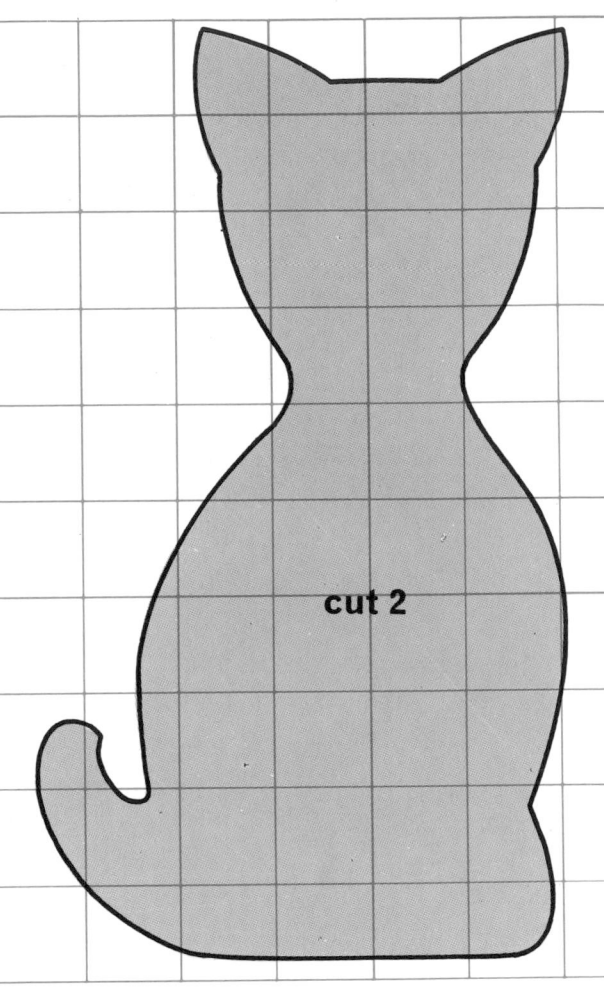

cut 2

Fig 9

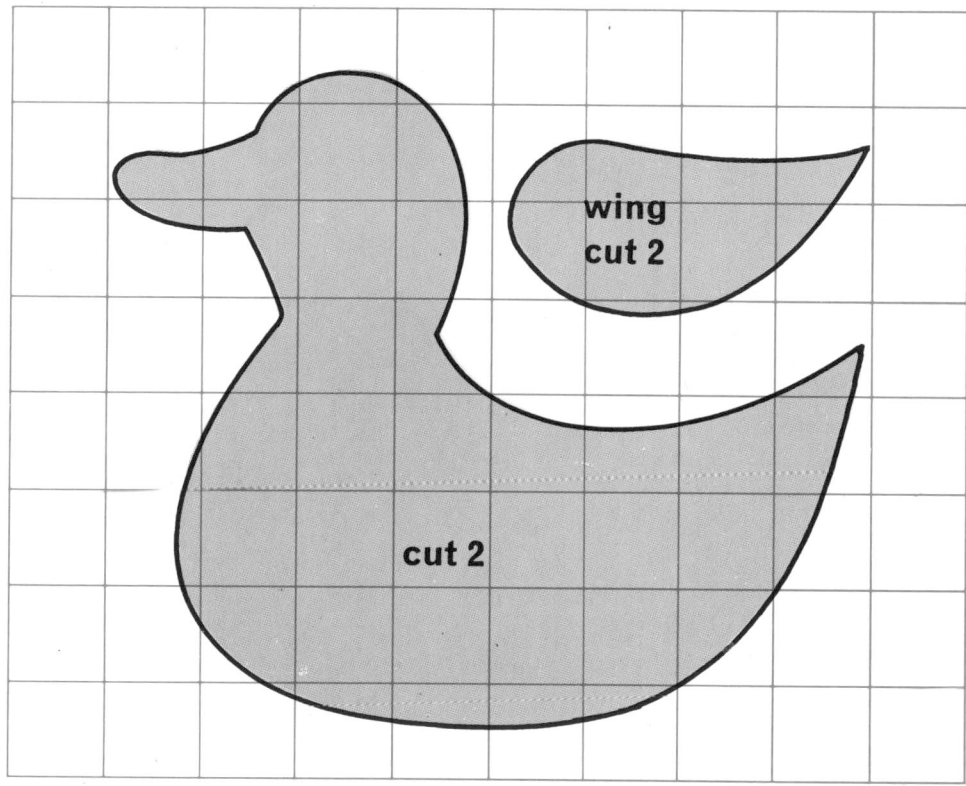

Fig 10

A duck

You will need:

A piece of orange felt measuring
21.5 cm by 35.5 cm (8½″ by 14″);
a small contrasting piece for a wing;
tiny piece of black felt for eyes; some
stuffing; embroidery silks; orange
cotton.

The beak is cut in one with the body, but
it can be cut separately if wished, in a
contrasting colour. Cut two body pieces
and two wings (Fig 10).

Embroider the wings in a feather design
in stem stitch or whipped running stitch,
pairing them for left and right sides (Fig
11). Sew them in place with invisible

Fig 11

stitches. Embroider a big, round eye with a
black centre, or sew on circles of felt.

Pin the two duck pieces together,
matching head and tail, and oversew,
starting at the tail, over the back, head and
beak. Fill the beak and head with small
pieces of stuffing. Continue sewing and
stuffing, leaving an opening in the under
seam, until the remainder of the body is
filled; then sew up the opening.

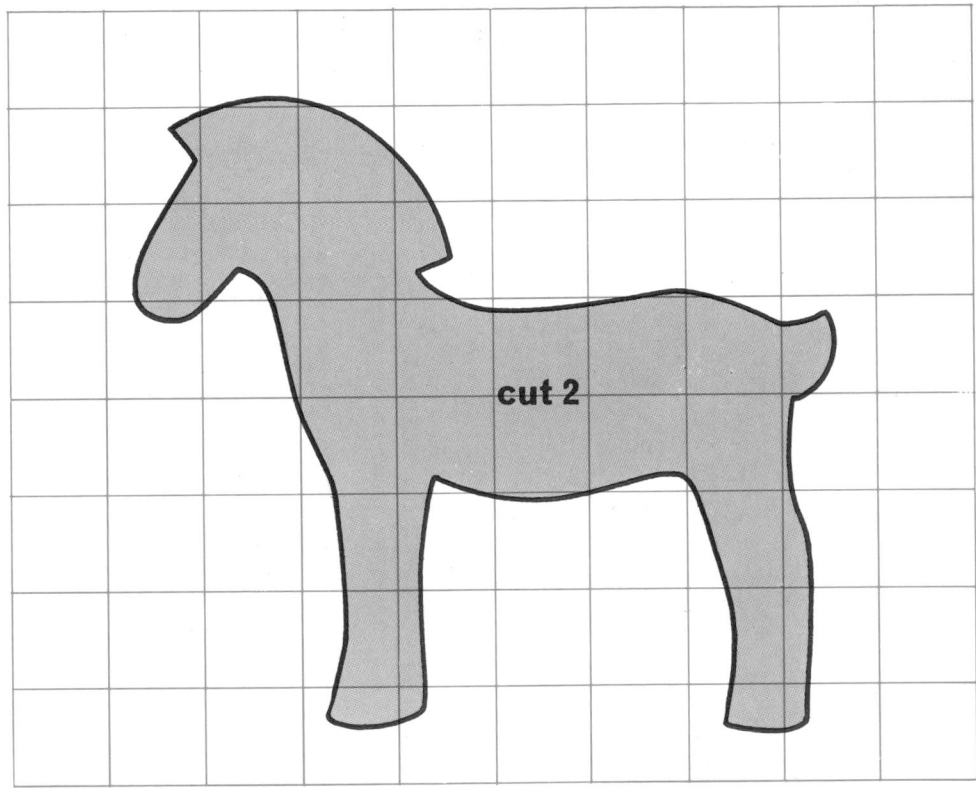

Fig 12

A little horse

The pattern is cut in one, with the mane and tail included, but they can be cut separately in contrasting colours and sewn in with the seams (Fig 12).

You will need:

A piece of felt measuring 21.5 cm by 35.5 cm ($8\frac{1}{2}$" by 14"); some stuffing; matching cotton; a strand of black embroidery silk.

Cut two pieces and pin them together, matching legs and head; oversew, starting at the inner seam of the front leg and stopping at the front edge of the mane. Stab stitch along the base of the mane, leaving the two edges free. Stop at the back of the neck. Stuff the front leg and head. Continue sewing along the back to the tail. Stab stitch along the base of the tail, leaving the two edges free. Sew the back leg and halfway up the inner seam, and stuff the foot. Finish sewing the rest of the inner leg seam and complete the leg stuffing. Stuff the rest of the body and sew up the under-body seam.

Embroider oval eyes slanting towards the nose, and the mouth. Cut the edges of the mane and tail into a fringe.

Strips of felt for a harness, and a saddle cloth in contrasting colour can be added if wished.

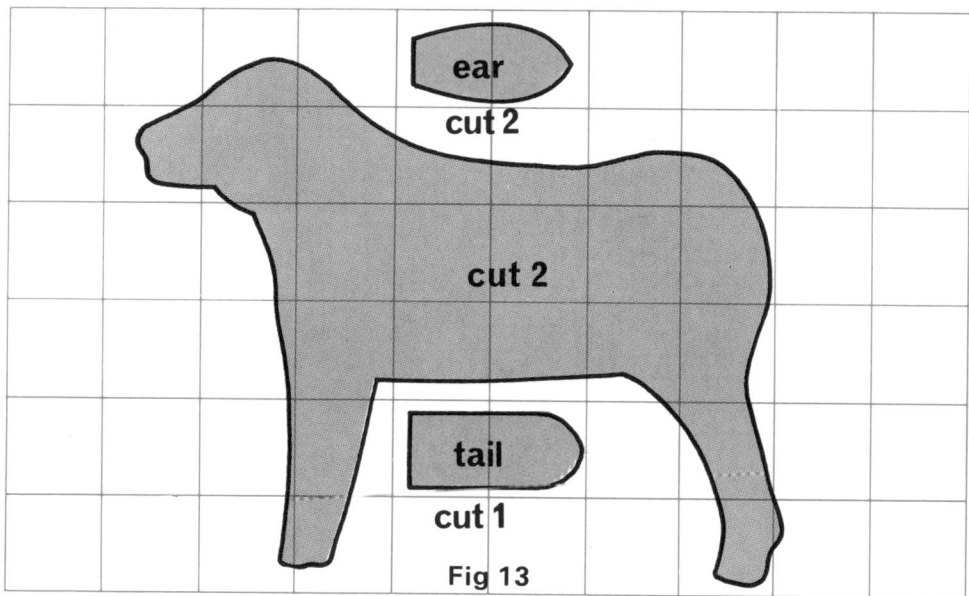

ear
cut 2

cut 2

tail
cut 1

Fig 13

A lamb

The pattern is of the head and body in one with separate ears and tail. This one is made from fluffy, white, man-made fibre, but any colour felt can be used (Fig 13).

You will need:

A piece of man-made fibre 19 cm by 28 cm ($7\frac{1}{2}$" by 11"); some stuffing; embroidery silk; sewing cotton.

Trace round the template on to the wrong side of the man-made fibre, pressing down firmly on the edges of the template to keep it in place. (Man-made fibre is usually stretchy, not firm like felt, so it will move under the template unless held fast and a bad shape will result.) Remember to reverse the template to trace the second side.

Cut a rectangle for a tail and two pointed ears.

Sew seams on the wrong side for man-made fibre. Pin the shapes together with the right sides inside and matching feet and head, and tack the edges. Oversew the edges firmly, using a locking stitch by putting the needle twice into the same hole. Start sewing from the inner seam of the front leg, round chest, head, back and back leg, fastening off at the top of the inner back leg seam. Turn it inside out and gently press the seams as flat as possible.

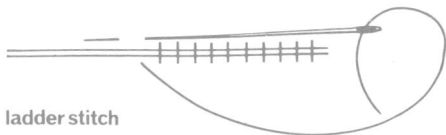

ladder stitch

Fig 14

a. single chain stitches

Fig 15

Stuff the head and legs, and then the rest of the body. Sew up the opening with ladder stitch (Fig 14), which is done by taking a stitch first in one side and then in the other and pulling the thread taut.

Fold the rectangle for the tail with the two edges together on the under side and sew them together, curving in the end.

Embroider yellow spots for the eyes with a ring of black back stitch round them and a nose and mouth in single chain stitches as in Fig 15. Fold the two corners of the ears to the centre and sew them on the head near the top, with ladder stitch, so that they stand away from the head.

If the lamb is made in felt it can, of course, be seamed on the right side.

A pet white mouse

You will need:

A small piece of white felt measuring 10 cm by 13 cm (4" by 5"); a strand each of pink and of white embroidery silk; some stuffing; some white cotton.

Cut out two pieces, reversing the pattern for the second one, and two ears (Fig 16).

Make a cord for the tail with the white embroidery silk — fold it in half and tie the ends. Pin one end down securely. Insert a pencil in the other loop and twist it until a firm, hard cord is obtained. Put the two ends together and the remainder will twist into a cord. Tie a knot in the end at the required length of the tail.

Sew the pieces together on the right side, starting to sew at the under edge of the front foot and over the head, stopping at the back of the neck. Stuff the front leg with very small pieces of stuffing, pushing it into place with a blunted orange stick, or cocktail stick. Stuff the head. Pin the tail in place with the knotted end inside. Sew the back, sewing in the tail with the seam, and round the back leg. Stuff the back leg with small pieces and then the rest of the body. Sew up the opening.

Embroider eyes and nose in close straight stitches in pink silk. Fold the corners of the ears to the middle (Fig 17) and sew in place on the head so that they point along the back. Whiskers can be sewn in with fine white nylon thread.

Fig 17

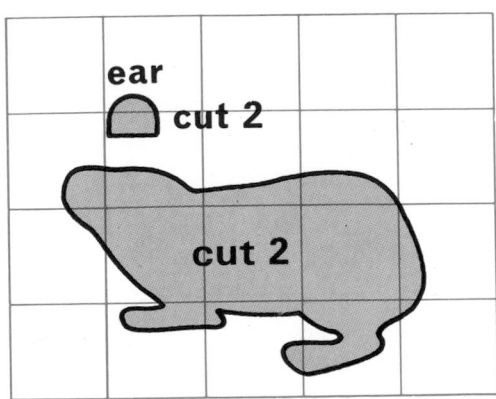

Fig 16

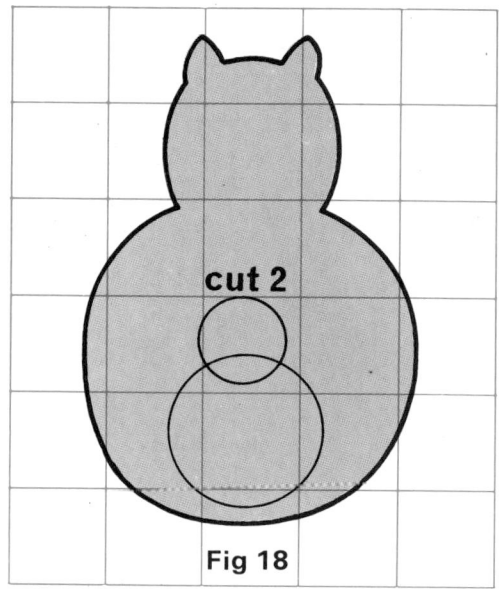

cut 2

Fig 18

Cats on elastic (for a pram)

Any of the previous toys cut to a smaller size can be threaded on a cord or elastic to amuse a baby as they jig about when strung across his pram.

You will need:

A small piece of different-patterned gingham for each cat; some bonded interlining for lining; kapok for stuffing; one or two pipe cleaners; a piece of round elastic.

Make a template for cutting out the cats by drawing a circle 10 cm (4″) in diameter, and overlapping the top of it a circle 5 cm (2″) in diameter (Fig 18). Draw two ears on top of the smaller circle. The lining should be cut 1 cm ($\frac{1}{2}$″) smaller all round (Fig 19).

For each cat cut out two shapes in gingham and two in interlining. Place the interlining shape in the centre of the gingham so that an even edge is left all round. Snip small 'v's out of the gingham edge so that the turning will lie flat (Fig 20).

Tack the gingham edge over the interlining. Repeat this with all the cat shapes. Place two pieces together with the right sides outside and sew all round the head and ears. Ease some kapok into the head in small pieces to make a rather flat finish. Continue to sew round the body, leaving an opening. Stuff the body through this opening.

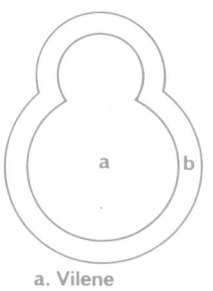

a. Vilene
b. gingham

Fig 19

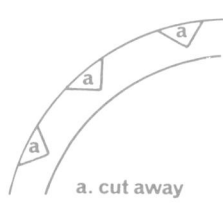

a. cut away

Fig 20

Cut off a piece of pipe cleaner about 5 cm (2") long and sew a strip of gingham round it for a tail. Sew this firmly to the back of the cat, curl it round to the front and sew in place.

Embroider eyes, nose and whiskers.

When all the cats are finished, thread the elastic through the necks from side to side and they are ready to be put on the pram.

The cats can be made rounder by lining a 1 cm ($\frac{1}{2}$") wide strip of gingham with interlining and sewing each side of the cat to it, being careful to match everything up. Fusible interlining also can be ironed on to the gingham cats and then no allowance need be made for turnings.

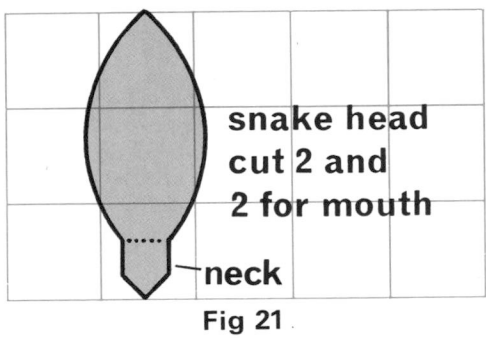

snake head cut 2 and 2 for mouth
neck

Fig 21

A wired snake

You will need:

A long, thin piece of green felt — this one measures 61 cm (24") from head to tail and is just over 1.25 cm ($\frac{1}{2}$") wide in the middle of the body (the head is cut separately); a small piece of orange or red felt for a mouth; two pieces of pipe cleaner chenille measuring 61 cm (24") and 7.5 cm (3") or these same lengths could be made from pipe cleaners twisted together; about 3 m (3 yds) of thin gold cord (the kind used for Christmas parcels); matching sewing cotton.

Cut two pieces of green felt 56 cm (22") long and 1.25 cm ($\frac{1}{2}$") wide tapering to 3 mm ($\frac{1}{8}$") at the tail, two pieces for the head (Fig 21) and two similar shapes in red felt for the inside mouth.

Oversew two of the long edges together, finishing at the tail. Sew along the second side, enclosing the long length of pipe cleaner as you go. Two inches will be left

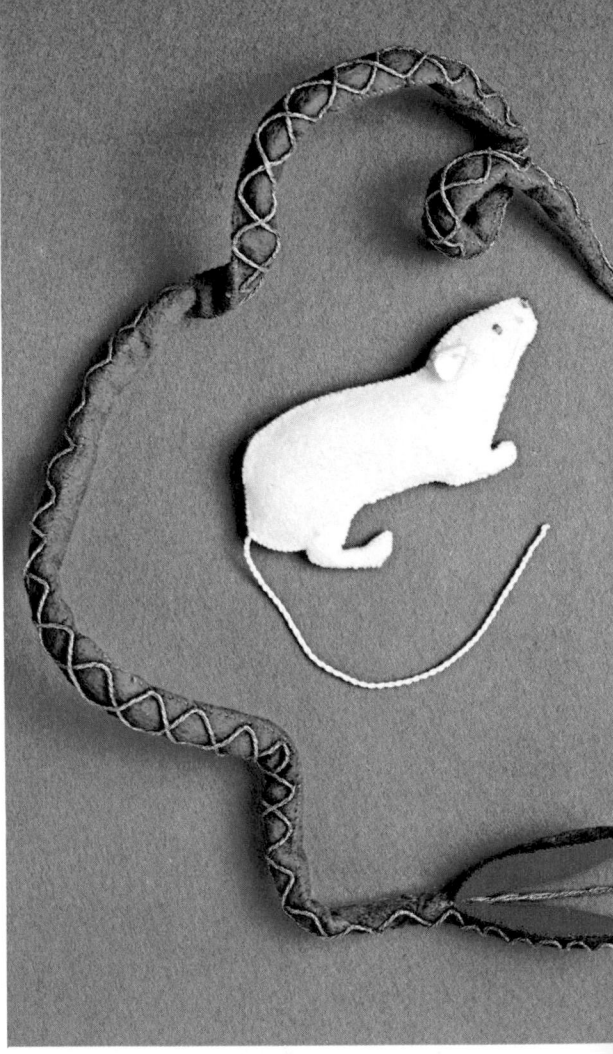

projecting from the neck. Cut off the neck from the inner mouth pieces, leaving about 3 mm ($\frac{1}{8}$") of it (Fig 22). Sew a red and a green piece together, enclosing the projecting end of pipe cleaner as the second side is sewn (Fig 23). Sew it on to the neck of the body piece, sewing the straight cut edge of the red mouth on to the straight edge of the neck of the body piece and the pointed arrow shape of

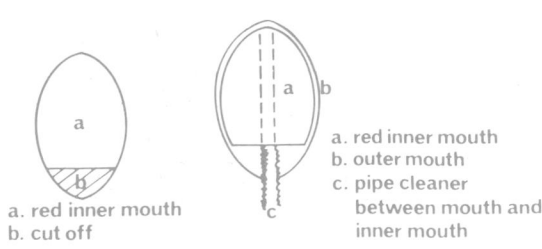

a. red inner mouth
b. cut off

Fig 22

a. red inner mouth
b. outer mouth
c. pipe cleaner between mouth and inner mouth

Fig 23

the end of the green piece down the back. Sew the other green and red pieces together, enclosing the short length of pipe cleaner when sewing the second side of it; sew it to the second side of the body in the same way, tucking the remainder of the pipe cleaner into the body.

Sew a twisted piece of gold cord to the back of the throat for a tongue. Sew the sides of the head together at the neck for about 1 cm ($\frac{1}{2}$"). Sew the gold cord all down the back in a diamond pattern. It can be made to seem to slither along by bending the wire, or coiled round with its head poised and alert.

A set of wired lengths

These can be twisted, bent and curved into dozens of different shapes and designs, both singly and several together.

You will need:

Many different-coloured pieces of felt about 1.5 cm ($\frac{5}{8}$") wide and in lengths from 7.5 cm (3") or 10 cm (4") to 60 cm (24") or 75 cm (30") or more if you wish (several lengths can be joined together to make rainbow lengths); pipe cleaner chenille cut in lengths, or pipe cleaners twisted together to give the required length.

Bend back the sharp ends of the wire to avoid them sticking through the felt. Cut the strip of felt about 3 mm ($\frac{1}{8}$") longer than the pipe cleaner. Fold the felt in half down its length and oversew the edges, enclosing the pipe cleaner as you go. Oversew the ends securely.

The picture shown has been made from wire lengths mounted on hessian-covered strawboard.

CHAPTER SIX

Toys with gussets

The flat two-piece toys described in Chapter Five can be made rounder and more solid by inserting gussets. These can be

(a) the straight strip kind with the body pieces sewn on each edge of it, or

(b) curved ones with pointed ends, inserted in the back or underneath or both, or

(c) cut to shape to form under-parts to legs so that the toy animal will sit or lie down or stand or walk.

If you make your own patterns or templates you can either draw or trace a side view of the animal in any position and add the appropriate gusset to it. The simplest one is (a) the straight strip gusset.

A dog

The dog shape has been simplified and the template (Fig 1) includes ear and tail in one with the body.

You will need:

Felt; kapok or other soft stuffing; embroidery silks; matching cotton.

Cut out two side pieces from your template, in felt, and cut a straight strip 1.5 cm ($\frac{5}{8}$") wide and long enough to go right round the edge of the felt body shape. If the strip has to be cut in sections, make the necessary joins at specific points: under the feet, at the top of the inner leg seams, under the body, under the chin, or on top of the ear or tail. Joins will be less noticeable in any of these places than in the middle of the back or on the nose.

Pin one edge of the strip all round one edge of the dog shape, being careful to pin exactly at corners like feet, tail, ear and nose. Pin close to the edges to avoid showing pin marks.

Oversew all round the edges.

Pin the second side to the strip, matching points at head, ear, tail, feet exactly with the first side, or the finished toy will be twisted.

Start sewing from the inner front leg seam over the head to the back of the neck. Stuff the front leg and head carefully, pushing stuffing into the corners and seams. Continue sewing along the back and the back leg. Fill the back leg and the rest of the body with stuffing and sew up the opening.

Embroider the eyes, nose and mouth with black embroidery silk and make a collar from a narrow strip of contrasting felt.

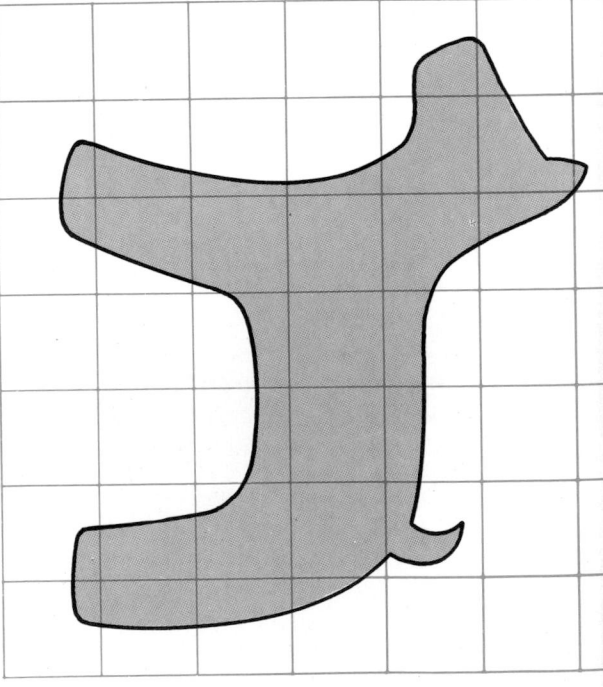

Fig 1

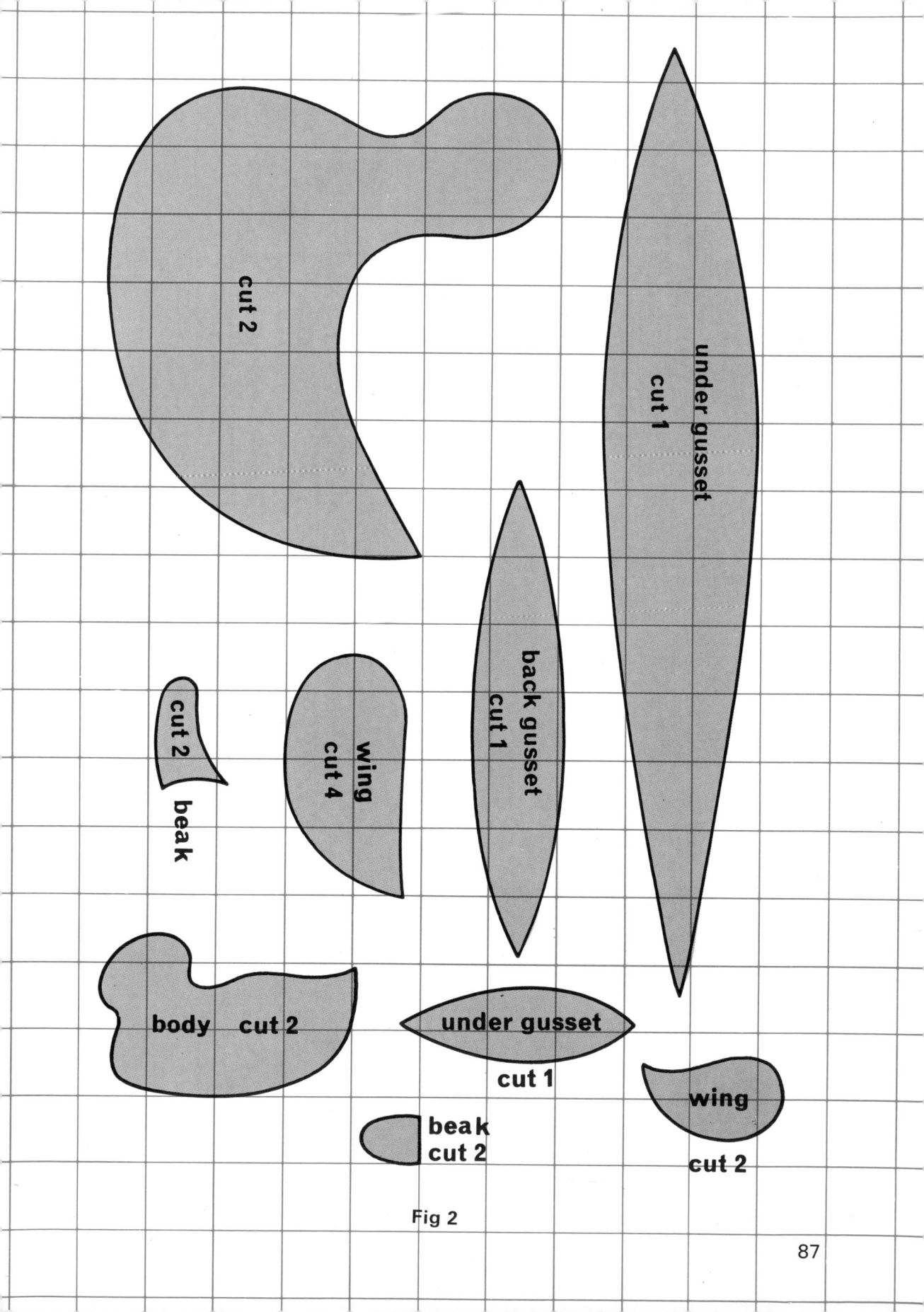

Fig 2

A duck and ducklings

You will need for the duck:

A piece of yellow felt 25 cm (10")
by 38 cm (15"); a small piece of orange
felt for a beak; some sequins;
embroidery silks; kapok or similar for
stuffing; matching cotton.

The template

The shape is fairly simple and it is easy to
make your own template (Fig 2). Draw or
trace a side view of the duck and make a
template of it in thin card. Cut another for
the beak and the wing. It has a curved
gusset in the back and a longer curved
one underneath. Measure along the curve
of the back from the back of the neck to
the tail (Fig 3). Draw the gusset this
length, tapering to a point at each end and
about 3 to 4 cm ($1\frac{1}{4}$" to $1\frac{1}{2}$") wide in the
middle. For the under gusset, measure
from the tail along the under-body curve
to just below the beak, and draw the
under gusset this length, the same shape
as the upper one, but 5 cm (2") wide in
the middle (Fig 3).

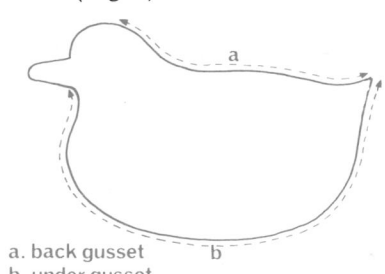

a. back gusset
b. under gusset

Fig 3

Fig 4

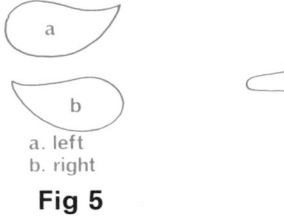

a. left
b. right

Fig 5   **Fig 6**

Cut out

Place the templates on the felt, starting
with the under gusset which will take the
full 38 cm (15") length. Cut one under
gusset, one upper gusset, two bodies and
four wings from yellow felt and two beaks
from the orange felt.

Embroider

Embroider two of the wing shapes for left
and right sides (Fig 5), both lower body
curves and tail and one-half of the under
gusset. Sew a ring of sequins round an
embroidered spot for an eye.

The beak

Oversew the curved edges of the beak, pad
it with a very little kapok, keeping it flat,
and sew in position on one side of the
head.

Make up

Sew both body pieces to the top gusset,
placing it, and starting to sew each time
from the tail. Sew one side of the under
gusset to the body. Oversew the head from
the top gusset to the under gusset. Pin
the second side to the under gusset,
starting at the tail and finishing exactly
under the beak. Start sewing from the
beak down the neck. Stuff the head
smoothly with small pieces of kapok,
pushing it in gently to the seams to keep a
good shape. Continue oversewing and
stuffing as you go, using small pieces and
keeping it free from lumps.

Sew a plain wing to an embroidered
one, leaving an opening for stuffing. Ease
in a little stuffing in small pieces keeping it
flat. Sew up the opening and sew the
wing in position with tiny invisible stitches
taken about 3 mm ($\frac{1}{8}$") below the edge of
the oversewing so that the edge of the
wing stands out a little from the body.
Repeat with the second wing.

Tie a thread round the neck to mark the
collar. Sew a ring of sequins on top of the
thread and embroider one or two rows of
coloured whipped or threaded running
stitch above and below it (Fig 6).

Fig 7

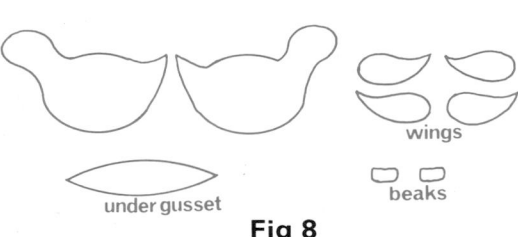

wings

under gusset

beaks

Fig 8

The ducklings

For each of them you will need:
Yellow felt 10 cm by 15 cm (4" by 6"); orange felt; beads; embroidery silks; cotton.

They are made from a similar type of template as the duck, but not so elaborate in finish. Draw two ovals, touching one another, one for the body about 7.5 cm (3") long and a smaller one touching it for the head (Fig 7). Draw two curving lines joining them for a neck, and add a small pointed tail. This will be the body template. Draw a small curved beak and a wing (Fig 8). The under gusset — there is no top gusset — stretches from near the chest to the tail. Draw one this length, about 2 to 2.5 cm ($\frac{3}{4}$" to 1") wide in the middle and tapering to a point at each end.

Cut out three or four ducklings to follow the mother duck, but cut out all the parts for one duckling at a time, making sure that it is complete. Cut two body shapes, four wings and one under gusset from yellow felt, and two beak shapes from orange felt.

Sew a few small beads on the front part of each body piece, and embroider two of the wing pieces. Sew on a sequin or a ring of beads for an eye.

Sew a plain wing and an embroidered one together, leaving a small opening. Ease in small pieces of stuffing, enough to pad it a little. Sew up the opening and sew it in position on the side piece with small,

invisible stitches. Repeat with the second wing.

Sew the curved sides of the beak together, ease in a little stuffing and sew it in place on one of the side pieces.

Place the two body pieces together and oversew the edges from the tail to under the beak. Sew one side of the under gusset to the body. Pin the gusset to the second side, matching it exactly with the first side. Start sewing from under the beak, down the neck and front of the body. Fill the head with small pieces of stuffing, and continue sewing, stuffing the rest of the body as you sew.

A hen and chicks

These can be made in the same way. The hen's beak is smaller and she would have a scalloped red comb on top of her head (Fig 9) — cut in two pieces, the scalloped edges oversewn and the whole then sewn in with the head seam. Two red wattles, one each side of the beak, hanging down below it each side of the neck, could be cut single or double in red felt. The chicks resemble the ducks but with much smaller, pointed beaks.

Fig 9

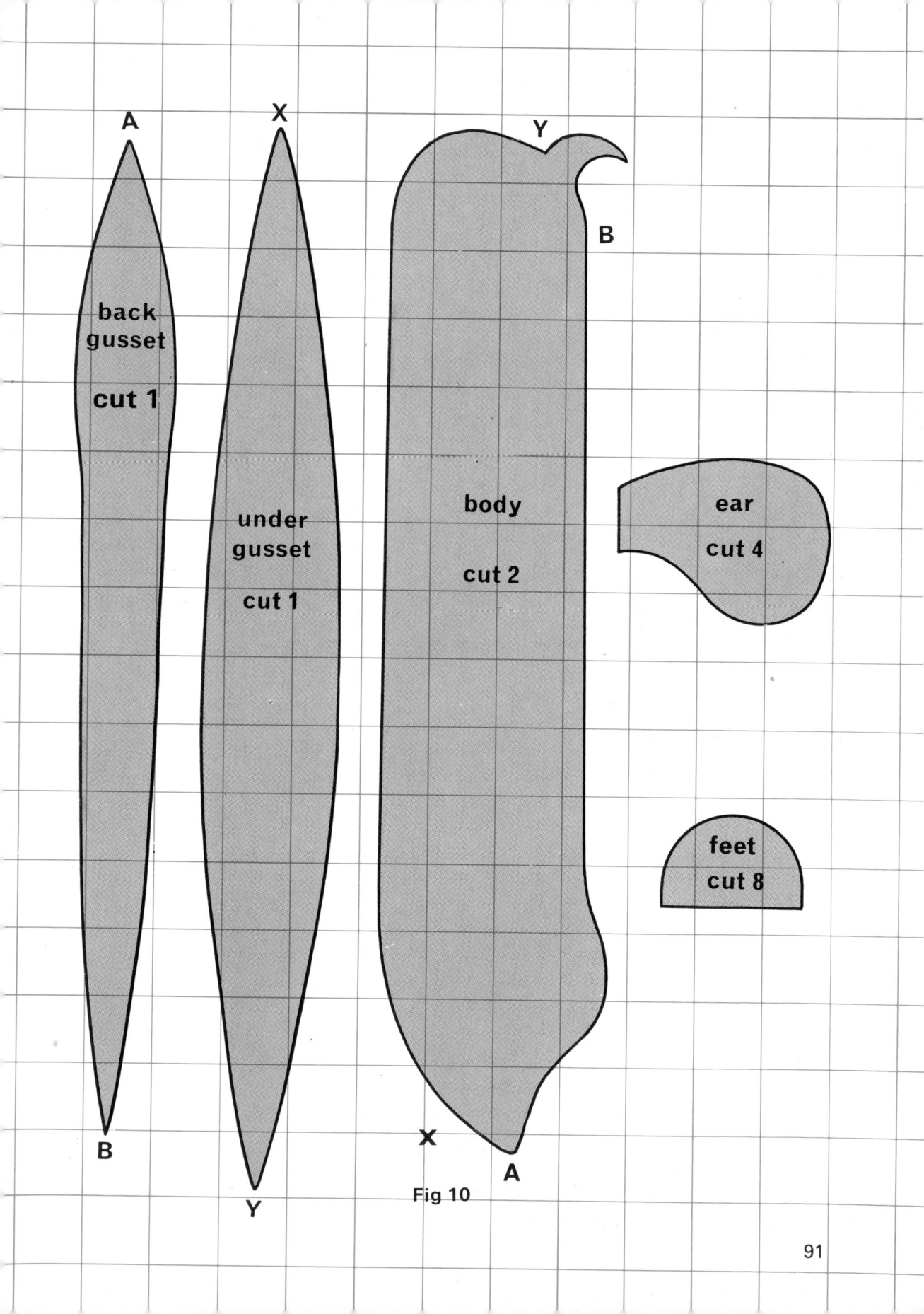

back
gusset

cut 1

under
gusset

cut 1

body

cut 2

ear

cut 4

feet
cut 8

A

X

Y

B

B

X

Y

A

Fig 10

91

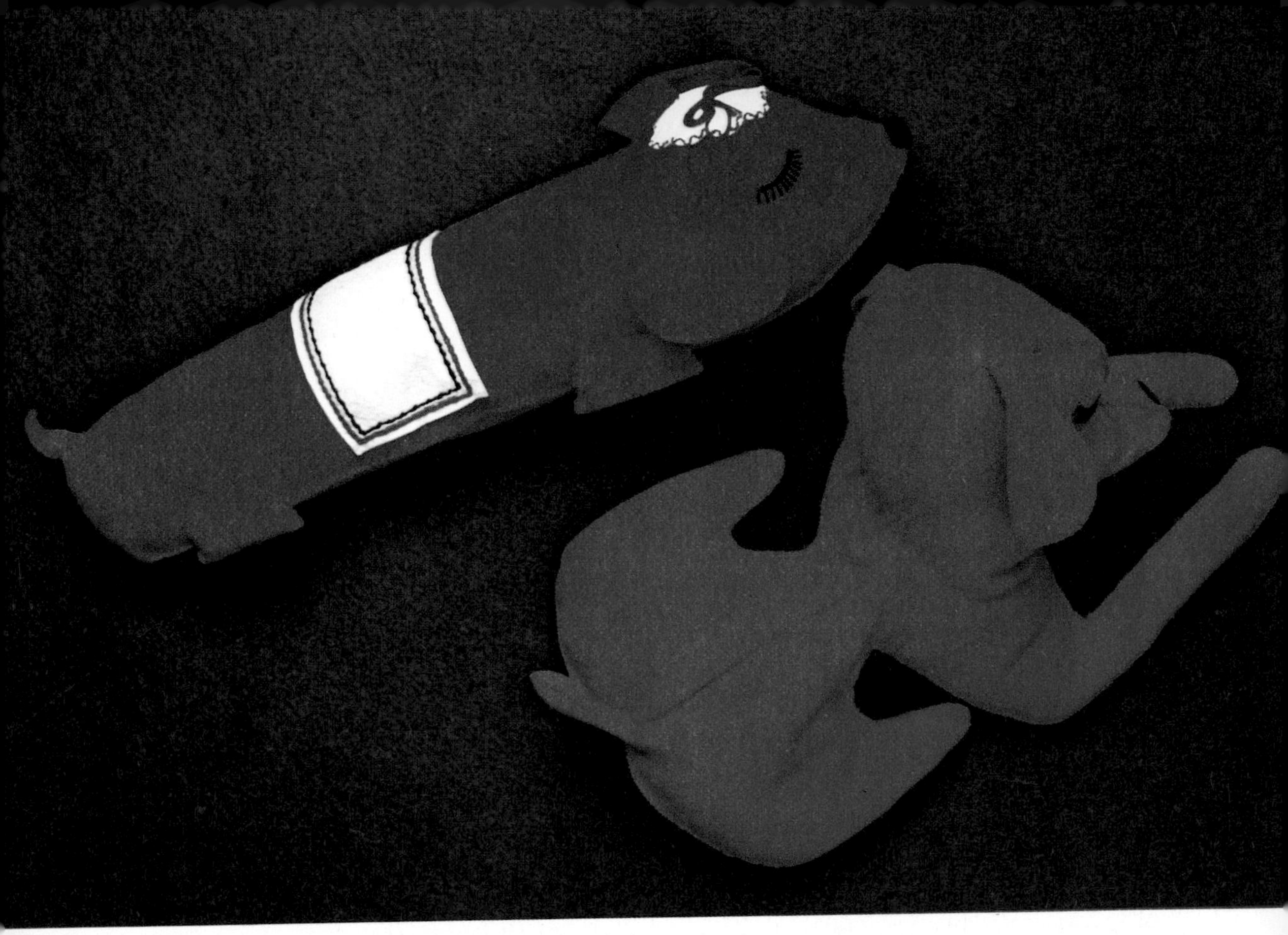

A sleepy dachshund

In a small size, like the one in the picture with the sleepy poodle (to make the poodle, *see* p 108), he is a cuddly, soft toy; twice as big, he will lie on the floor along the bottom of your door and keep out all draughts.

You will need:

A piece of felt 38 cm by 38 cm (15" by 15") for the body; a rectangle of contrasting colour for a coat; some embroidery silk, including black; matching sewing cotton; some kapok for stuffing.

He can be most easily made in felt. Any closely woven material can be used, but in this case remember to leave 1 cm ($\frac{1}{2}$") turnings when cutting out the pieces. If thinner material is used then an inner lining of something like unbleached calico should be made.

He is fairly easy to draw for making a template (Fig 10) because the outline has been simplified and the body is almost a sausage shape.

There are back and under gussets. For the under gusset measure the curve under the body from 5 cm (2") below the tail to the nose, and cut the gusset this length, tapering at both ends and measuring 5 cm (2") in the middle. The back gusset is different because the widest part comes at the top of the head. Measure the length from the nose over the back to 2.5 cm (1") from the tail and mark where the top of the head comes. The widest part here should be 4 cm (1$\frac{1}{2}$"), then tapering gently to a point at the tail end and more sharply to the nose so that the face part

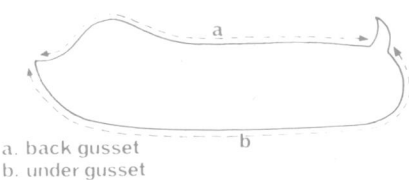

a. back gusset
b. under gusset

Fig 11

head

Fig 12

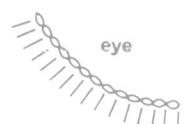

eye

Fig 13

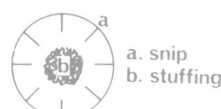

a. snip
b. stuffing

Fig 14

will be triangle shaped (Figs 11 and 12). The ears are shaped like a stubby boot and the legs are semi-circular.

Cut out two body pieces, four ears, eight legs, one back gusset and one under gusset, and a rectangle in contrasting felt long enough to cross over his back and about 6 cm (2½") wide. He will be about 38 cm (15") long when finished.

Sew the two sides to the back gusset, taking care to match nose and tail so that the second side matches the first, and starting the sewing from the nose each time. Put in any pins right on the edge so that stitching will cover up the marks. Sew one side to the under gusset, starting from the nose. Pin the second side in position and start sewing it from the nose end. The two sides, under and back gussets should meet in a point at the nose.

Sew about a quarter of the gusset and then stuff the head. Push the kapok gently into the point of the nose and into the head seams to keep a good shape. Continue sewing and stuffing and sew the remainder of the under seam, over the tail and the back.

Features

For the eyes, embroider a crescent shape in black chain stitch with straight stitches radiating from it for eye lashes (Fig 13). Either embroider a nose in embroidery silk or cut a small circle about as big as a 2p piece, snip the edges, place a small ball of stuffing in the centre and gather up the edges (Fig 14). Sew this on over the point.

Sew together two ear pieces round the curved edges for each ear. These are padded softly and flat in shape. Sew on to the seams just behind the widest part of the head with the 'toe' of the 'boot' pointing towards the nose.

Sew together two leg pieces round the curved edges for each leg, pad softly and flat and sew in position on the body so that the straight edges rest on the floor. Check that each side matches.

Embroider round the edges of the rectangle for the coat and sew it in place on the back.

To make him into a draught excluder, double his length and make his width half as much again.

A wise old owl

You will need:

Felt for the body, for wings and eye surrounds; some soft stuffing like kapok; embroidery silks.

His shape has been made simple so that he can be easily drawn or traced (Fig 15). His head and body are made rounder by inserting gussets, and the wings and feet are added separately when the seams are sewn. The one in the picture is made in chestnut-coloured felt with beige wings and eyes and bright orange feet.

Templates

Trace the pattern pieces on to thin card and trace round them on to the felt, reversing the pattern where necessary to keep all pencil marks on the wrong side.

Cut out two body pieces in the chestnut felt; four wings, two oval eye surrounds in beige felt, two circles in orange felt (drawn round a ½p piece), two smaller ones in white and two slightly smaller in black for the eyes; two gussets in chestnut felt, one for the head which will stretch over the head from one side of the neck to the other, and the other one for the base; and four feet shapes from the orange felt. A scrap of black makes the diamond-shaped beak with one rounded end (Fig 16).

Embroidery first

Embroider a pair of wing shapes for left and right with scattered brown fly stitches (Fig 17). For the eyes, sew a black circle to a white one and sew both on to an orange circle. Place them in the centre of an oval of beige and fasten this down with long, black straight stitches radiating from the edge (Fig 18). They should be

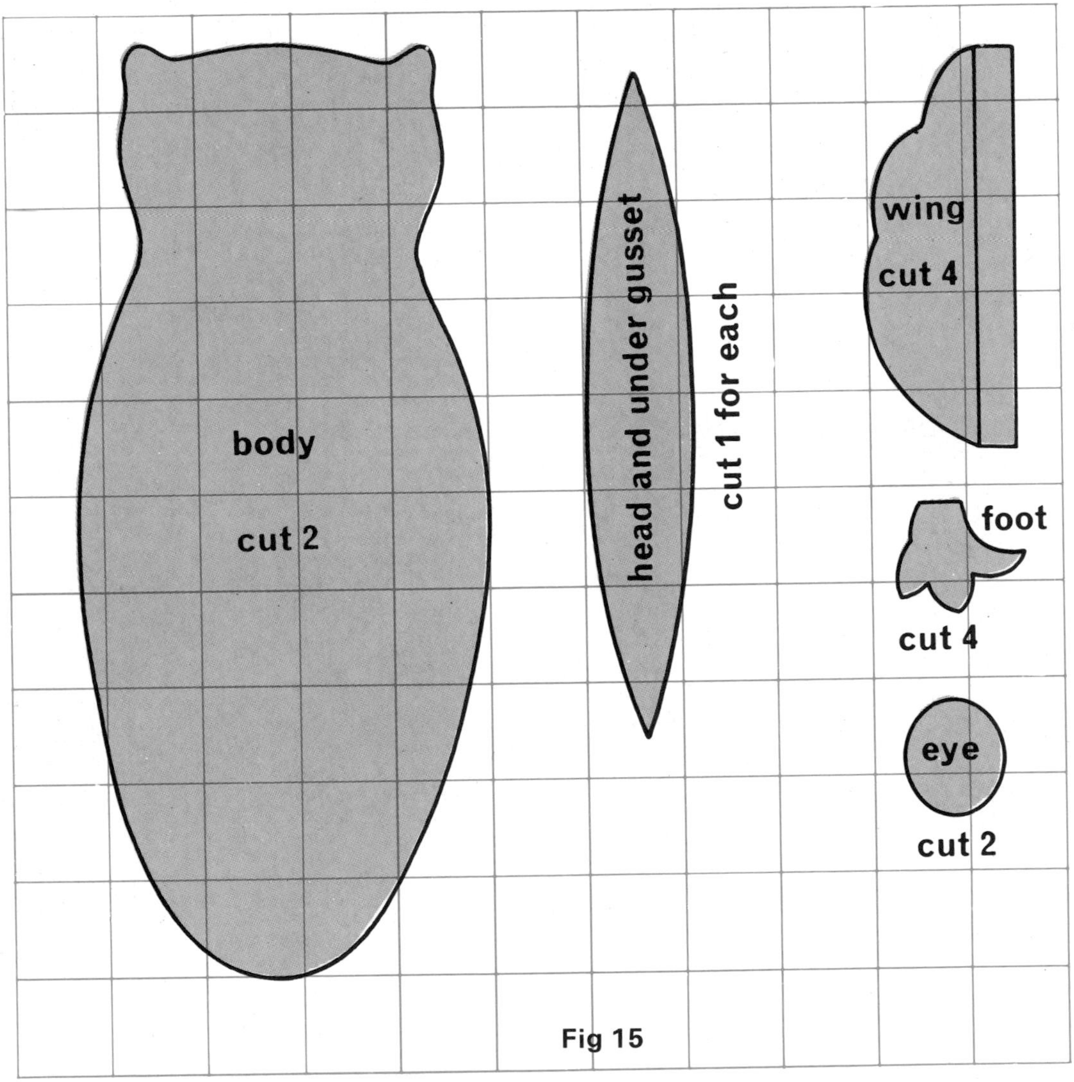

body

cut 2

head and under gusset

cut 1 for each

wing

cut 4

foot

cut 4

eye

cut 2

Fig 15

quite close together on the face. Embroider one of the body pieces below the neck in slanting lines of blanket stitch in yellow and brown (Fig 19).

Sew a triangular beak between and slightly below the eyes. Sew the two corners A and B (Fig 16), curving slightly in towards each other so that the pointed beak stands out from the face.

Sew a plain and an embroidered wing piece together round the curved edges and pad it softly to be slightly round but not hard. Then do the same for the other wing, and sew them on to each side of the front, matching the position of each, with

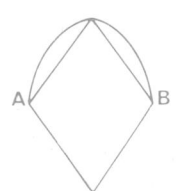

Fig 16

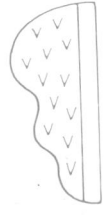

Fig 17

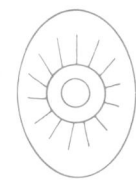

Fig 18

94

Fig 19

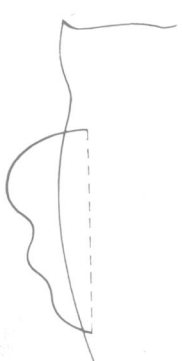

Fig 20

the wider part of the wing at the top (Fig 20).

Sew two felt pieces together for each foot, leaving the tops open. Stuff them with tiny pieces of kapok, pushing it gently and firmly into each claw and making the whole claw fairly hard. Sew them in position on the front piece.

Mark the centre of the top gusset edge and the centre of the top of the head, and pin the gusset in place, starting from the centre marks. Check that the points of the gusset match on each side of the neck. Oversew the edges.

Repeat with the back body piece.

In the same way mark the centres of the base edge and the gusset and pin in place, checking the position of the gusset points. Sew it in place, including the feet in the front seam. Sew the side seams of the body as far as the base gusset, including the wings in the seam.

Stuff the head, easing the stuffing into the ears and the seams, so that a good shape is made. Stuff the body. Sew half of the remaining gusset seam and complete the stuffing. Sew up the rest of the seam.

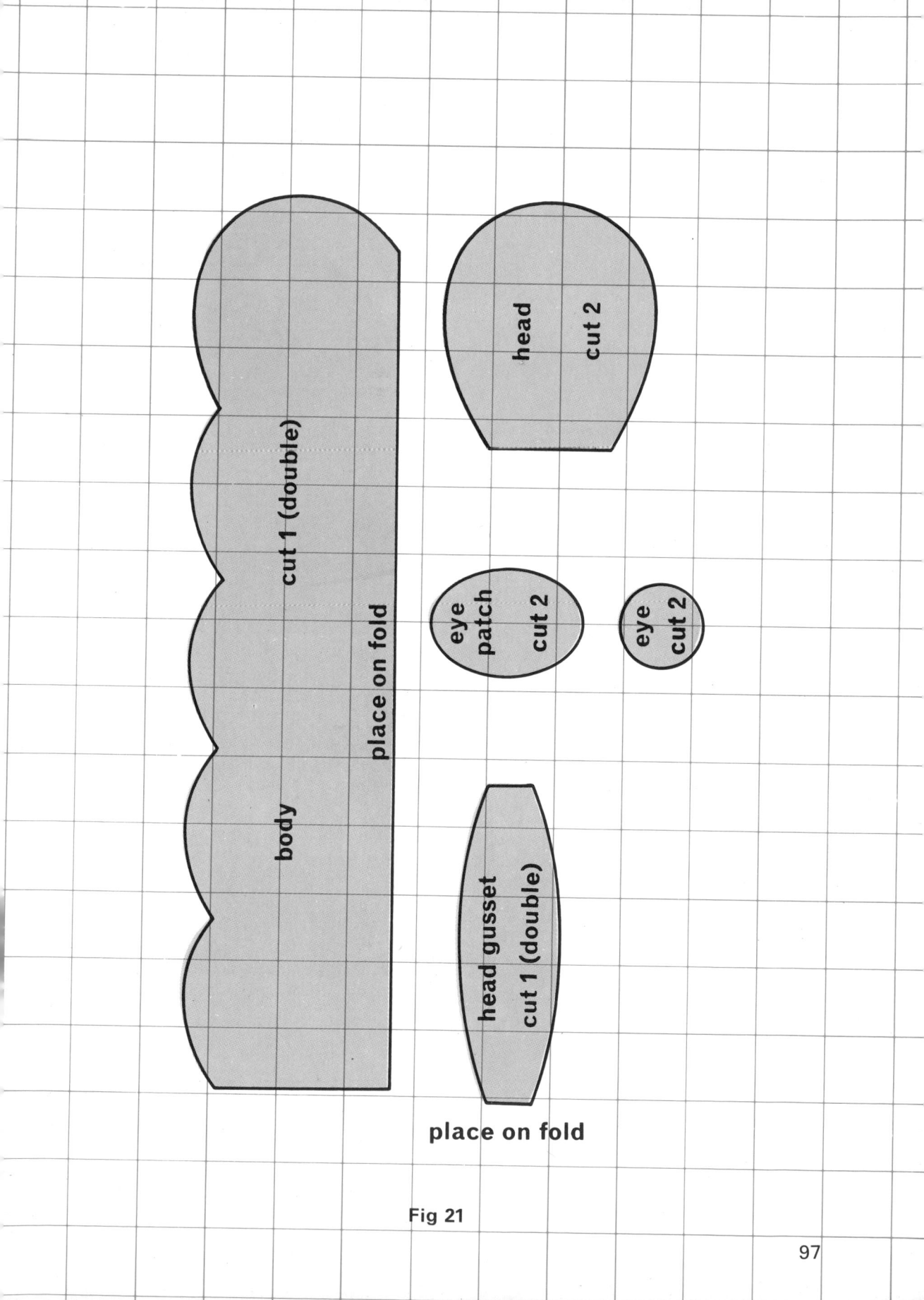

Fig 21

97

A colourful caterpillar

You will need:
Felt; kapok; cotton; black embroidery silks.

He, like the dachshund, can be a cuddly toy or, made longer and fatter, will lie along the bottom of the door and keep out the draughts. He is made from green felt, a piece 33 cm by 15 cm (13" by 6") and has an orange and yellow felt head, with circles of black and white felt for his eyes.

Trace the pattern shapes (Fig 21) on to thin card and use as templates.

Cut out one body piece, two head pieces in orange, one head gusset in yellow, two black and two white circles.

Sew a black circle on to a white circle with the edges touching on one side (Fig 22); repeat for the other eye. Sew them in place on each head piece, close to the rounded edge which is the front of the head, with the eye looking forward (Fig 22a).

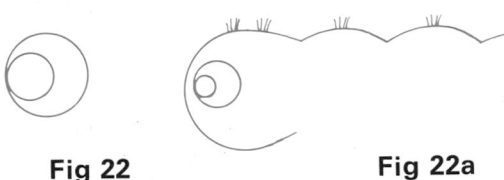

Fig 22   **Fig 22a**

Mark the centre of the curve in the head pieces and pin them to the head gusset, the narrow part of the gusset to the centre of each head piece. Sew them in place.

Fold the body piece in half and oversew the tail and the scalloped edges, leaving the front open.

Stuff the head firmly for a smooth, round shape and fill the body, pushing the kapok well down into the tail with a blunted pencil. Pin the head to the body, with the scalloped top of the body pinned to the middle of the head gusset edge. Sew them together with ladder stitch (Fig 23) — that

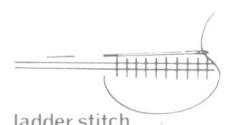

ladder stitch

Fig 23

is, one stitch in the head and one stitch in the body, pulling the thread together fairly tight. Push in any extra stuffing before closing the seam.

Work a row of yellow wool tufts all along the back on both sides of the seam and a ring of them on the top of his head. The tufts are made by threading a needle with a double strand of wool and then taking a stitch in the felt, leaving an end. Take a second stitch across the first and draw the end of wool and the needle through the loop, pulling it tight (Fig 24). Cut off the ends.

Cut two strips of felt 2 cm ($\frac{3}{4}$") wide and the length of the body. Cut out notches in one long side of each and sew them along the length of the body so that the notched side touches the floor, resembling feet.

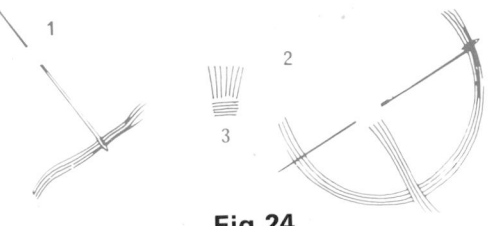

Fig 24

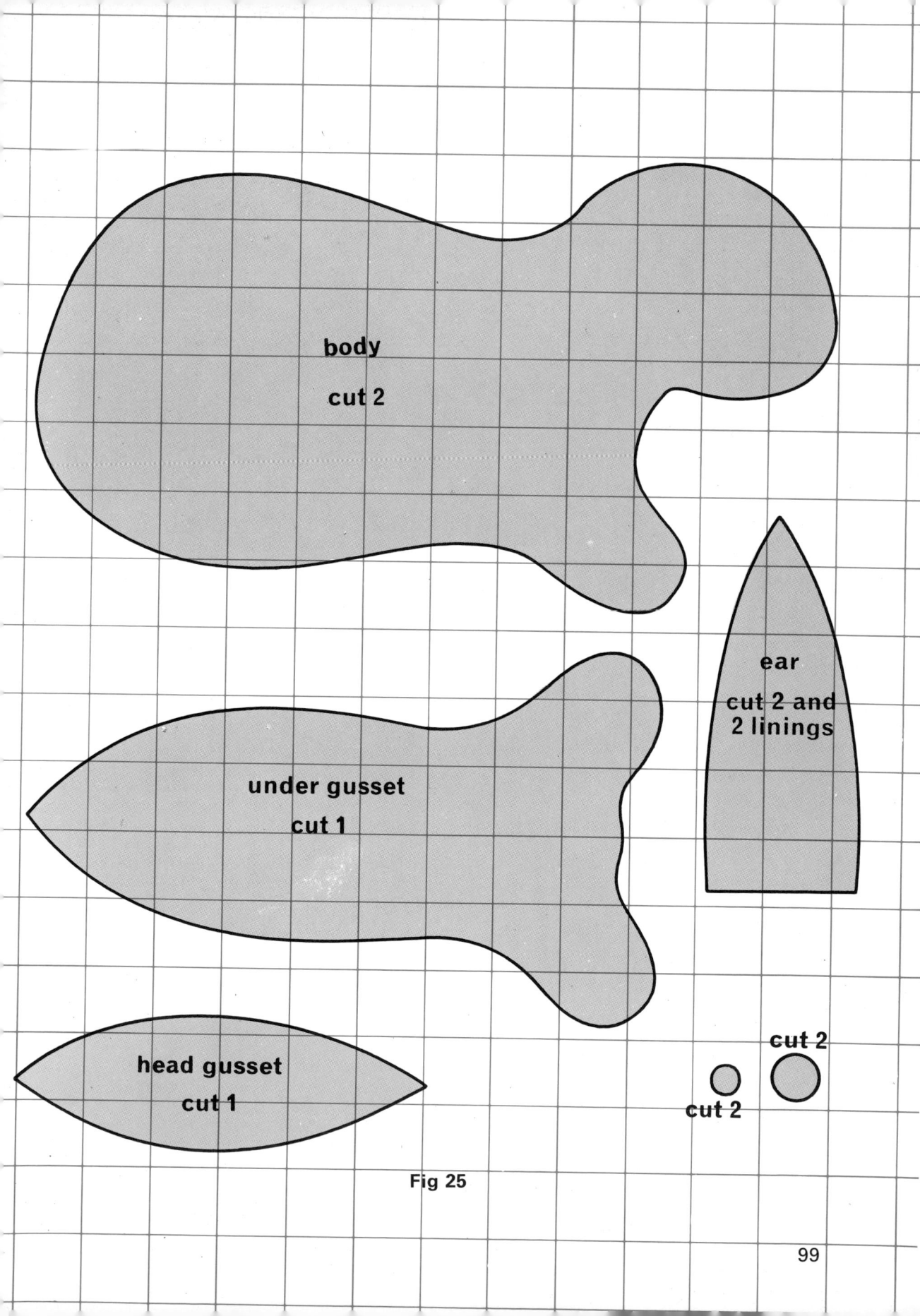

body

cut 2

ear

cut 2 and
2 linings

under gusset

cut 1

cut 2

head gusset

cut 1

cut 2

Fig 25

A white rabbit

She is a pet rabbit sitting with one ear down and one ear up, listening and waiting for her little owner to bring her a crisp lettuce leaf. She has an under gusset to make her sit nicely and a head gusset to make the head rounder (Fig 26).

You will need:

White, fluffy, man-made fibre 30 cm by 50 cm (12" by 20"); pink felt for the ear linings; soft, fluffy wool for the tail; kapok or similar stuffing; scraps of pink and black felt for eyes; a strand of black embroidery silk; some soft, white wool.

The template is made from the silhouette of a sitting rabbit (Fig 25). A line drawn from below the tail to the middle of the chest gives the shape of half the under gusset. The head gusset stretches from the point of the nose to the back of the neck. The widest part of this is not quite in the middle, so that it comes at the top of the head; it is 6 cm ($2\frac{1}{2}$") wide and tapers to a point at each end.

The ears are about 14 cm ($5\frac{1}{2}$") long and are leaf-shaped.

Trace the patterns on to thin card and trace round them on to the wrong side of the man-made fibre. Press down hard on the edges because the material stretches easily and will move about under the card unless held very firmly.

Cut two body pieces, one under gusset, one head gusset and two ears out of the man-made fibre, two ears from the pink felt, two pink circles drawn round a 2p piece, and two black ones, slightly smaller, for the eyes.

The sewing is done on the wrong side. Sew both pieces to the head gusset, starting each time from the nose and stitching with double oversewing, that is, taking two stitches into the same spot each time. Sew the under gusset to one side in the same way.

Pin the under gusset to the second side, but do not sew it.

Sew the front seam on the chest, from the nose to the gusset, and the back seam from gusset to gusset.

Take out the pins and turn the rabbit inside out. Sew in the under gusset as far as the paw. Use ladder stitch on this seam, taking a stitch first in one side and then in the other.

Now fill the head with small pieces of stuffing, keeping it smooth and free from lumps, and a good shape. Continue sewing, stuffing as you go.

Sew a pink felt ear to the right side of a man-made fibre ear, leaving the straight side open. Turn it inside out and press out the seam. Repeat with the second ear. Fold the points into the centre and sew them on at the top of the head on the seam, using ladder stitch. Press one ear down as you sew it.

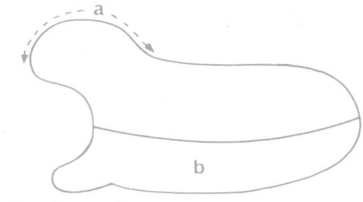

a. head gusset
b. under gusset

Fig 26

Fig 27

Sew the black felt circles on to the pink ones and sew them on to each side of the head on the gusset seam.

Sew the nose and mouth in black embroidery thread in single chain stitch (Fig 27). Sew a few whiskers on each side.

Lay a double strand of white wool along a piece of card 2.5 cm (1") wide and wind the white wool round both card and strand of wool 30 to 40 times. Cut the loops of wool and tie round them tightly with the double strand over which they were wound. Trim the ends to make a fluffy ball and sew it on at the back where the under gusset ends.

The Three Bears

In chestnut-coloured felt with pinkish-coloured fronts, the three bears are a nice cuddly family to please any small child. Father Bear is twice as big as Baby Bear and half as big again as Mother Bear.

You will need:

A fairly large piece of chestnut-coloured felt (a 50 cm (20") square should be big enough); a smaller piece of the lighter colour felt for the fronts; scraps of yellow and of black felt; two or three strands of black embroidery silk; chestnut-coloured cotton; kapok or similar for stuffing; a card template.

Trace off the three patterns on to thin card and cut them out. Each bear needs the same number of similarly shaped but different-sized pieces to make it, and it is wise to cut out those bigger ones for Father Bear first (Figs 28, 29a and 29b).

After the pieces are cut, put them into polythene bags, label them and check all the pieces when you have finished cutting out. For each size you must cut two side pieces, a head gusset (Fig 28), which is more shaped than the head gussets have been up to now, four ears from the chestnut felt, two under-gusset pieces from the pinkish felt, two circles of yellow felt, two smaller black ones, and a black shield-shaped nose.

Sew the head gusset to both side pieces, the more shaped end of it being the face part. Sew each time from the nose. Join the two curved edges of the under gusset on to the wrong side and sew it to one of the side pieces matching up the paws. Sew together the nose and front neck seam as far as the beginning of the under gusset. Sew the back seam from the head gusset down to the tail end of the under gusset.

Fill the head, pushing stuffing well into the nose and cheek seams, but do not stuff too hard. Stuff the two paws which are sewn.

Pin the under gusset to the second side, matching the paws, start sewing from under the chin and complete the first paw. Stuff the paw. Continue sewing, stuffing the body as you sew. Stuff the back paw, pushing in any extra stuffing needed in the body and sew up the opening.

Sew together two ear pieces for each

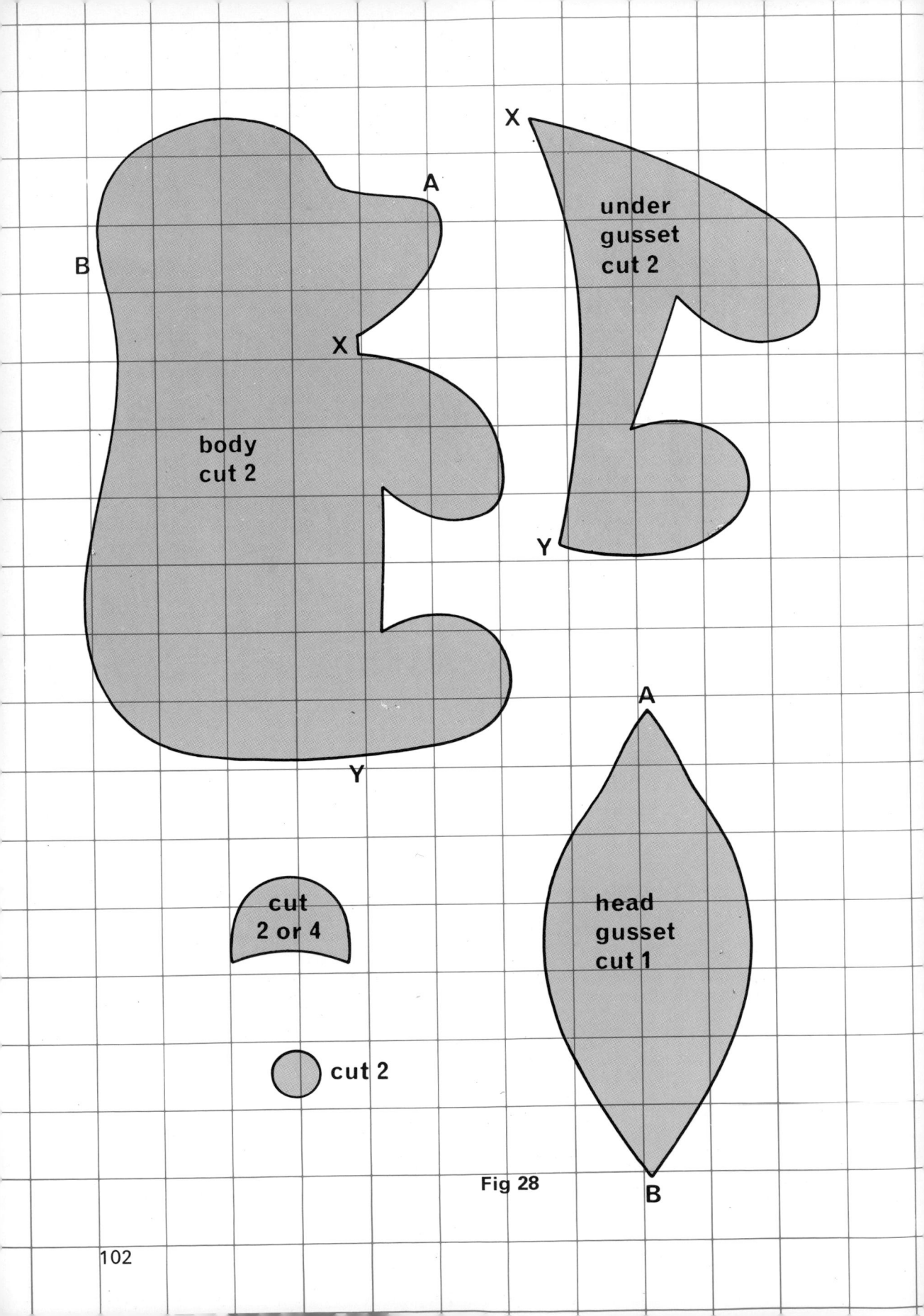

under
gusset
cut 2

body
cut 2

head
gusset
cut 1

cut
2 or 4

cut 2

Fig 28

102

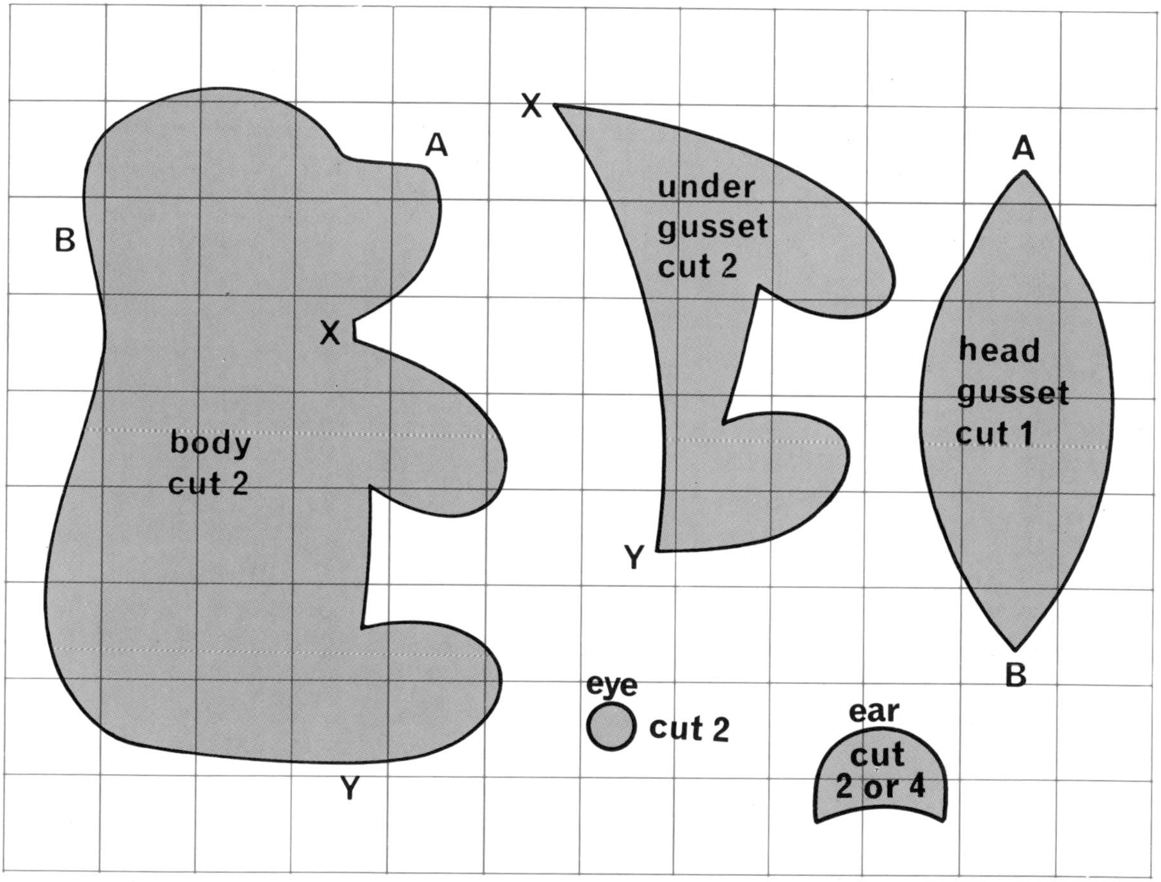

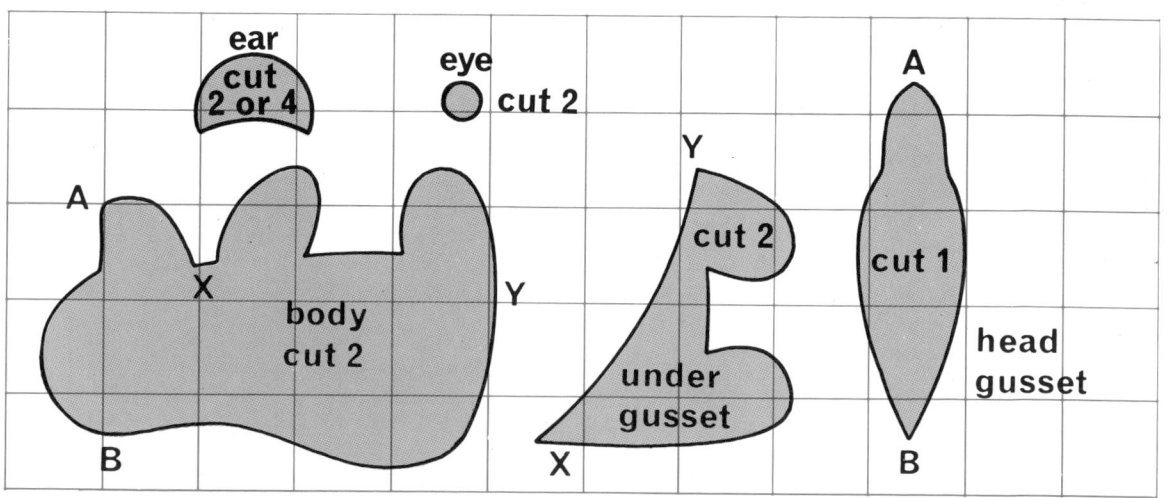

Fig 29a

Fig 29b

ear and sew them on to the side of the head in a horseshoe curve, the top edge on the head gusset seam. Use ladder stitch — taking a stitch in the ear and in the head alternatively.

Sew a black circle on to a yellow circle for each eye, and sew them on each side of the face.

Sew the black nose in place and embroider two lines in black chain stitch curving away from the bottom of it, for the mouth.

Embroider black straight stitches on the outside of each paw for claws.

Each of the other bears is made up in the same way.

A baby sea-serpent

She is very colourful in her violet, blue and green, and her sharply pointed, rose pink ears which seem to be listening. She is pictured on p 98.

You will need:

Violet-coloured felt for her two sides (a 30 cm (12") square will be sufficient); green felt for the under gusset; royal blue felt for the head gusset; bright pink felt for the ears; orange, yellow and black felt pieces for eyes; kapok or similar for stuffing; sewing cotton; black embroidery silk.

This, being an imaginary animal, can be as fanciful as you wish and the silhouette drawing for the pattern does not need to have a likeness to anything, but can be a combination of several animals.

Make a template in thin card (Fig 30) for the shape of the side, and shape the under gusset as before, by drawing a curved line about 1 cm ($\frac{1}{2}$") above the under-body curve. The head gusset is more elaborately shaped to make an interesting head shape, the broad muzzle narrowing into a waisted effect before swelling out into a rounded, rather dome-shaped head. This is achieved by measuring the length needed — from the middle of the nose curve where the mouth would be — to the back of the neck, and marking three places: the widest part of the nose, the narrowest part of it, and the top of the head. Draw the gusset curve accordingly, tapering both ends to a point, a gradual one at the back of the neck and a sharper one over the nose (Fig 31). The whole figure could be made rounder by continuing the gusset all along the back to taper off at the tail, but that might spoil the shape of the humps. Draw a long leaf shape for the ear, and three graduated circles for each eye, the largest round a 1p piece.

Cut two body pieces, one under and one top gusset, two ears in bright pink, two circles in orange, two smaller in yellow and two smaller still in black felt.

Sew the black circles on top of the yellow ones and both on top of the orange ones, all to one side of the orange circle (Fig 32), and sew them in place on the

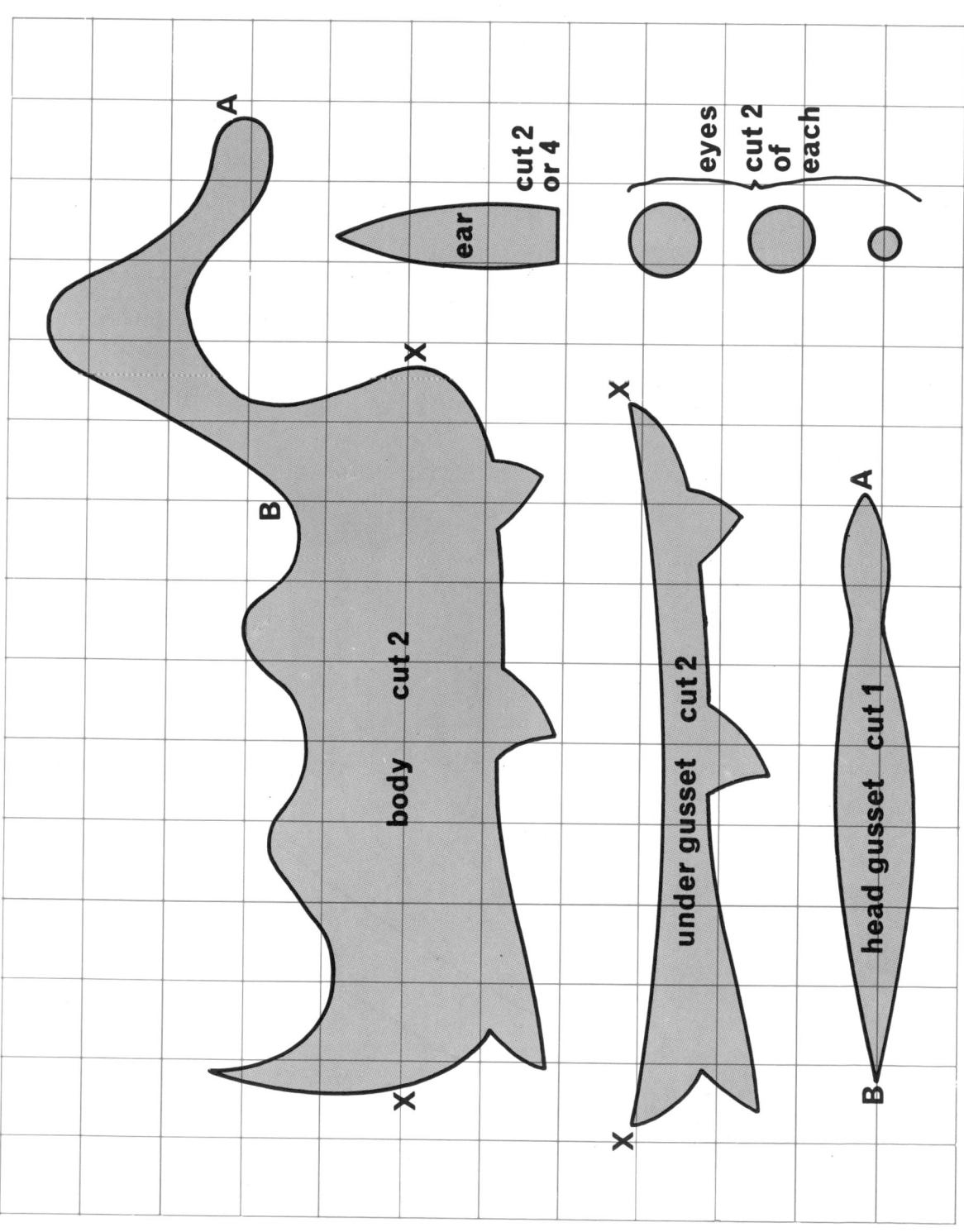

Fig 30

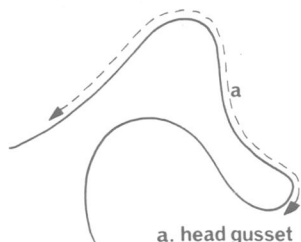

a. head gusset

Fig 31

Fig 32

sides of the head, looking down towards the nose.

Sew the top gusset to the two sides, being very exact about matching up the curves, and sew one side to the under gusset.

Sew the seam under the nose and chin for about 2.5 cm (1") and then stuff the nose very firmly, using small pieces to get a good shape. Continue sewing the seam an inch at a time, stuffing as you sew. It is important not to sew too much at a time. Stuff the flippers which are already sewn.

Sew the second side to the under gusset, stuffing the body as you sew and keeping it softer than the neck.

Fold the corners of the ears to the centre and sew them on top of the head on the gusset seam so that they stand upright.

Cut two wavy green felt strands and sew them on under the jaw for a beard.

Two single chain stitch nostrils in pink and some black embroidery silk whiskers complete the sea monster.

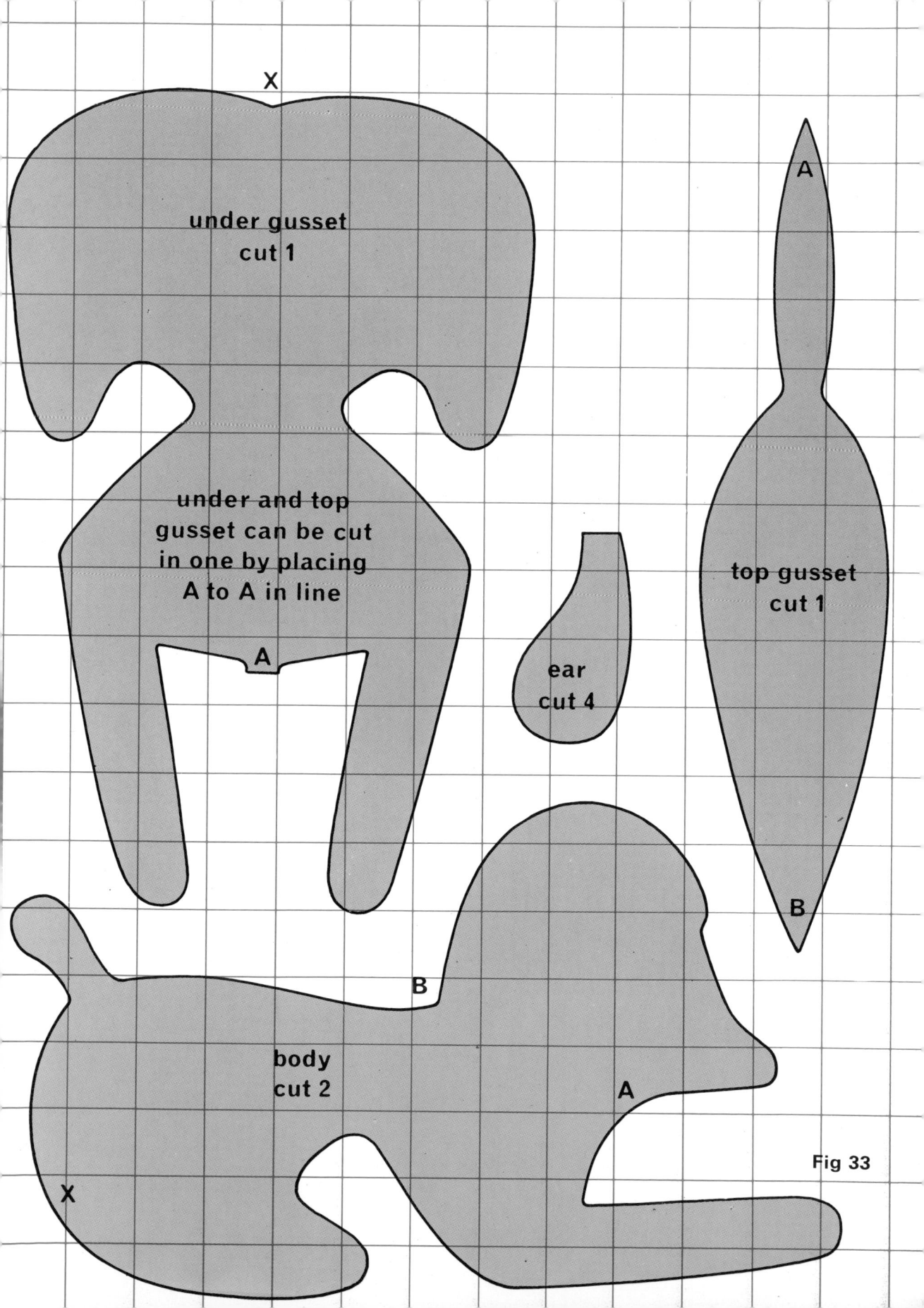

X

under gusset
cut 1

under and top
gusset can be cut
in one by placing
A to A in line

A

ear
cut 4

A

top gusset
cut 1

B

B

body
cut 2

A

X

Fig 33

A sleepy poodle

He is relaxed, his nose droops down to his paws and his eyes are closed. Shh! His photograph is on p 92.

You will need:

A piece of rose pink felt about 46 cm (18") square; kapok; matching cotton; black embroidery silk; black felt for nose.

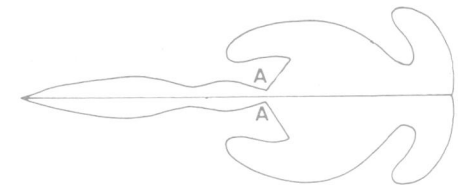

Fig 34

The pattern (Fig 33) shows a rather domed head, to simulate the height of a topknot. The side pieces are cut from a side-view silhouette and the under gusset of the lower part from a line drawn across the middle of the side piece from just below the tail to below the chin. The tail is included in one with the body piece.

The head gusset is shaped to form a nose and narrow face, and stretches from the back of the neck to underneath the chin. Here it is joined to the under gusset (Fig 34). It is a great advantage if the two gussets can be cut out in one piece, avoiding the join under the chin. To do this, draw lines right through the centre of each gusset and lay them on the felt with point A on the upper gusset joining point A on the under gusset and making sure that the two centre lines on them are in one continuous straight line. Cut out two body pieces, either one upper and one lower gusset, or one complete gusset, and four ears.

Pin the gusset to one side piece, matching paws and nose, and oversew the seams. Sew the back seam, over the tail, from one gusset to the other.

Stuff front and back legs which have been seamed, pushing kapok right into the corners but keeping them soft and not hard. Pin the gusset to the second side piece and sew, starting from the back of the neck over the head to the top of the chest.

Now stuff the head with small pieces of kapok, pushing it gently into the seams and particularly into the nose to make it firm but not hard, and keeping a good shape. Continue sewing round the front leg and stuff it, too. Finish sewing the remainder of the gusset round the back leg, stuffing as you sew.

Sew two ear pieces together for each ear, leaving the straight side open. Push a little kapok in to pad it softly, keeping a flattish look. Sew the straight edges to the gusset seam at the top of the head with the curved shape towards the nose.

Embroider a crescent-shaped line in chain stitch for each eye with a few straight stitches for lashes.

Cut a small shield shape in black felt and sew on the tip of the nose.

Kanga and little Roo

Kanga sits up very nicely and Roo makes himself comfortable in her pouch.

Roo is a rather flat shape made from two pieces, so that he fits easily into the pouch. Kanga has a head gusset and an under gusset which makes her a plump, well-fed looking kangaroo. She is 30.5 cm (12") high and her baby 6.5 cm (2½").

The pattern for Kanga is Figs 35 and 36. Roo's pattern is Fig 38.

You will need:

A piece of felt 30.5 cm by 61 cm (12" by 24"); some scraps of black and pink felt for eyes and nose; a strand of black embroidery silk; matching cotton; some kapok.

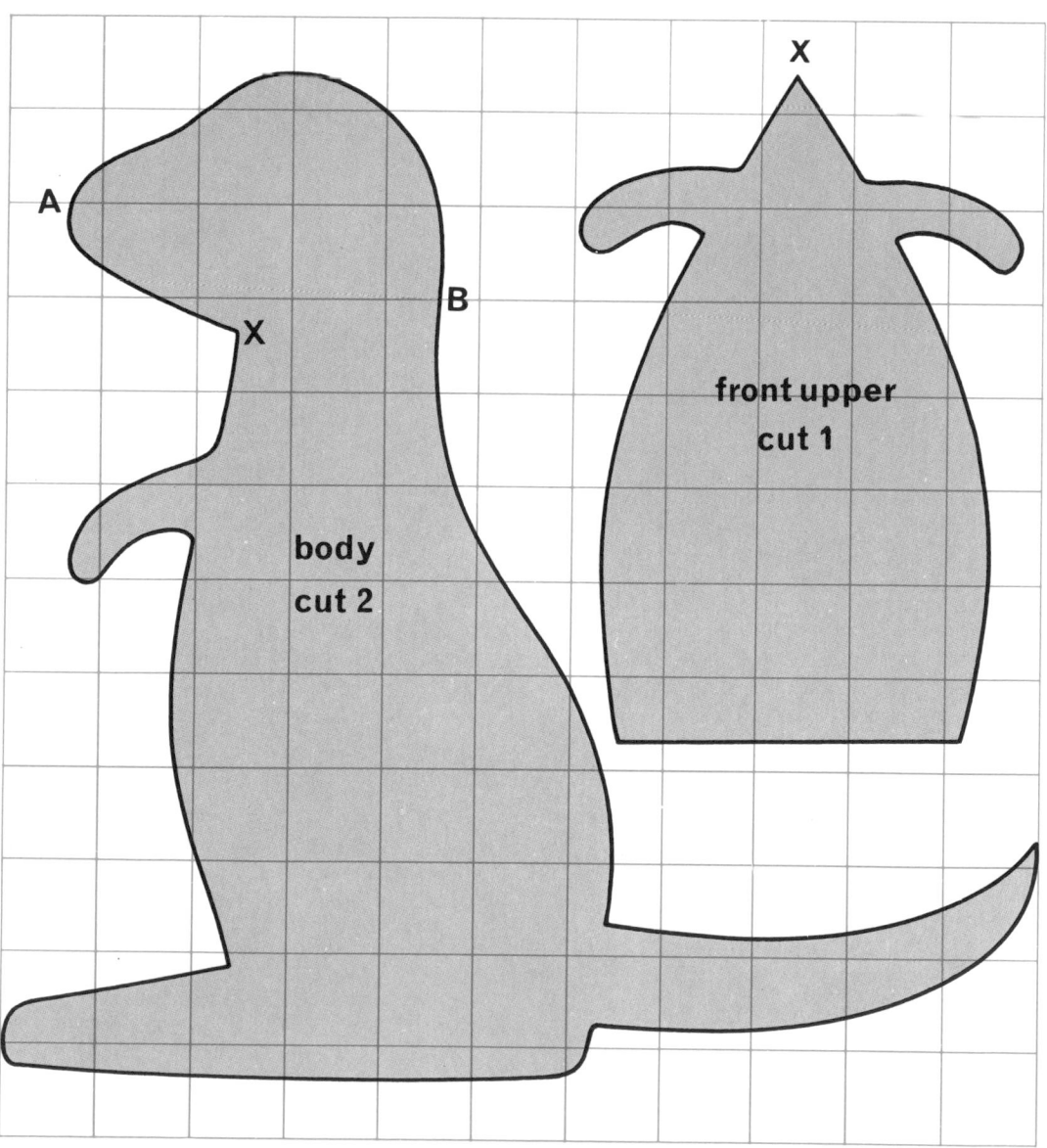

Fig 35

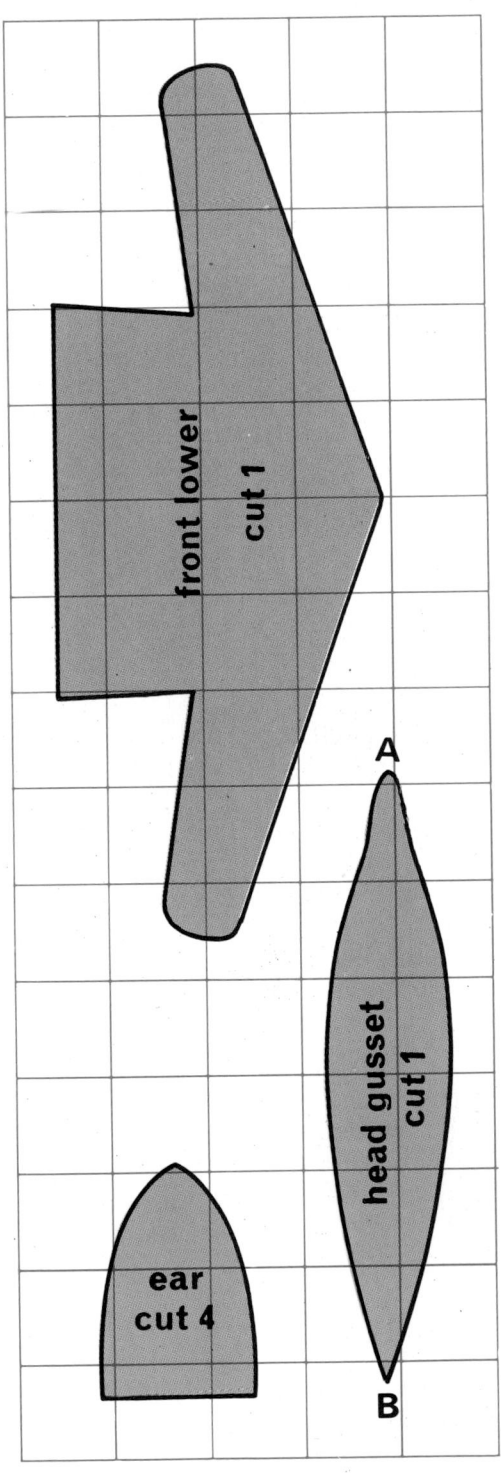

front lower
cut 1

A

head gusset
cut 1

B

ear
cut 4

Fig 36

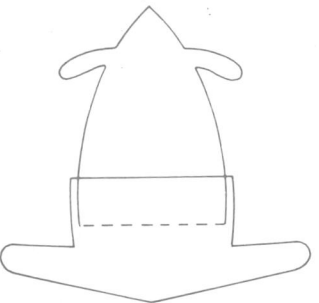

Fig 37

The under gusset is cut in two pieces, the lower part overlapping the top to form the pouch (Fig 37). Trace the pieces from templates in thin card, which have been made from the pattern.

Cut two side pieces, one head gusset, one under gusset in two pieces, and four ear pieces, all from the large piece of felt; a shield-shaped nose and two small circles for eyes from the black felt.

Sew the head gusset in place on both side pieces from the nose to the back of the neck. Sew the top part of the under gusset to both side pieces, matching up the little forearms. Sew the seam under the chin from nose to under gusset.

Stuff the head and the little forearms very firmly and stuff the forearms particularly with very small pieces of kapok, pushed in place gently with a blunted orange stick.

Pin the lower half of the under gusset in place, matching up the hind legs, with the straight edge overlapping the upper half.

Start sewing from this edge over the upper part of the gusset seam and continue round the back leg for about 2.5 cm (1") and then stuff it. Continue sewing the leg stuffing as you sew. Finish off at the back edge of the gusset. Repeat this with the second side of the lower gusset.

Sew the back seam, starting from the back of the neck and sewing halfway to the tail. Stuff the upper part of the body. Sew the rest of the back, and round the tail for about 2.5 cm (1"). Stuff this bit of tail and stuff the body. Continue sewing the tail about an inch at a time, stuffing very firmly. Push any extra stuffing needed into the body and sew the rest of the seam.

Sew together two ear pieces for each ear, fold the corners to the centre and sew

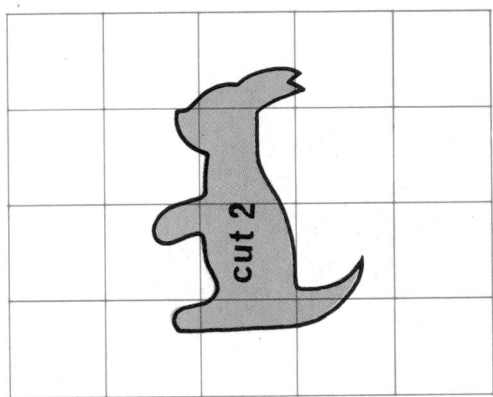

cut 2

Fig 38

them in place on the seams at the top of the head with the folds outwards. Use ladder stitch for fixing them.

For the eyes, cut two pointed ovals in pink felt, sew circles of black in the centre of them and sew them on along the gusset seams.

Sew on a shield-shaped piece of black felt for her nose and embroider a curved mouth in stem stitch.

For Roo:

Trace round the template twice (Fig 38) and sew the two pieces together, starting at the ears, down the back and round the tail. Stuff the tail. Sew on round the hind leg and stuff; round the front leg and stuff; then the lower part of the body, keeping it flat rather than round. Sew to the top of the head and stuff, then sew the rest of the ear, easing in the stuffing at the same time.

Embroider spots for the eyes and a little smiling mouth in stem stitch.

A penguin

He is smart in his traditional black and white with a brilliant orange flash above the eye, which is a shining black encircled with yellow. His beak is curved and down-pointing, the underside being yellow (Fig 40).

You will need:

Black felt; white felt; small pieces of orange and yellow felt; a strand of yellow embroidery silk; kapok; a piece of firm wire for the feet; sewing cotton; two large or twelve small black sequins.

The pattern is more involved than any up to now, and the front gusset is quite a different shape. It is really the front half of the body and does not include the feet. The flippers have a 6 mm ($\frac{1}{4}$") extra allowance down the straight sides for insertion in the seams.

The pattern pieces are as follows: the head; back and tail in one piece; the complete shape of the front; the flipper; eye patch; eye; head gusset; foot; two beak pieces, one the whole beak and the other the upper beak; and the triangular base. He stands 28 cm (11") when finished.

Trace all the pattern pieces and cut them out in thin card. In black felt, cut out two back pieces, four flippers, two upper beaks and four feet. In white felt, cut out the complete front in one piece. Cut two orange flashes and two yellow whole beaks.

Sew the orange flashes on to each head piece with the point at the cheek and the rounded part curling up to the top of the head (Fig 39). Sew a big black sequin or two rings of small sequins in place in the curve of the orange flashes for eyes. Work a ring of yellow chain or stem stitch round them.

eye flash

Fig 39

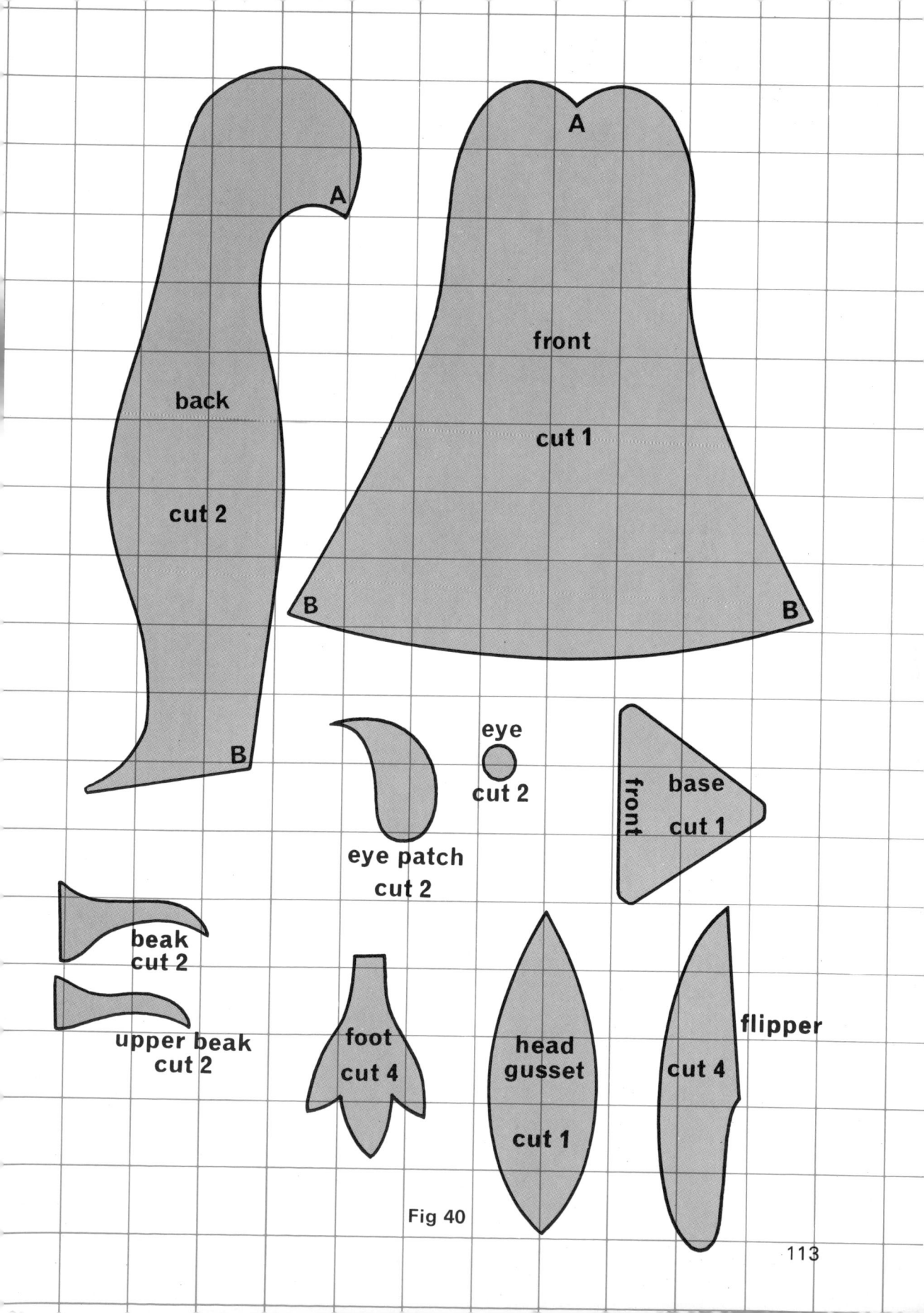

A

A

front

cut 1

back

cut 2

B

B

B

eye
cut 2

front base
cut 1

eye patch
cut 2

beak
cut 2

upper beak
cut 2

foot
cut 4

head
gusset

cut 1

flipper

cut 4

Fig 40

a. pipe cleaner chenille
wire shape for foot

Fig 41

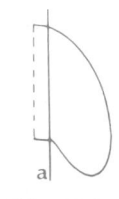

a. side seam

Fig 42

Sew the head gusset on to the side pieces.

Sew together two flipper pieces for each flipper and push in a little stuffing to pad them softly. Pin them in place with the edge of the back piece pinned on to the small flap allowed for a turning, so that the flipper stands out from the back.

Twist each end of the wire into shape to fit into the feet, leaving the middle of it in a loop which will be buried in the body (Fig 41). Sew together two feet shapes round the toes for each foot and push the wire in through the opening so that a 'toe' of wire fits into each felt toe. Push in some stuffing, keeping them fairly flat, and sew up the rest of the side seams.

Pin the front gusset in place, starting at the neck and taking great care to match the top curves; keep all pinning on the edge because of pin marks showing on the white felt.

Sew the gusset seams, sewing in the flippers as well (Fig 42). Stuff the head firmly, keeping a good shape.

Sew down the back seam a little at a time, stuffing as you sew. When halfway, pin the feet in position on the front, bending the feet at right angles at the toes and pinning at the top of the ankles. Continue sewing the back seam and stuffing, packing the stuffing round the wire to bury it in the middle of the body. Push the stuffing gently but firmly into the point of the tail. Push in any extra stuffing needed to make the base firm.

Sew on the triangular base piece, starting with the front, stitching in the feet very firmly from both sides.

Sew the black and yellow beak pieces together. Sew the curved seams all round, stuffing when sewing the second curve, and making it very firm. Stuff firmly right up to the opening, which should be kept open and should be oval in shape. Using ladder stitch, sew the beak on to the face, yellow side down and keeping the oval shape at the end. Take care that the beak is held at right angles to the face all the time you are sewing, otherwise it may turn to one side or the other and spoil the effect.

He should stand quite well, balancing on feet and tail.

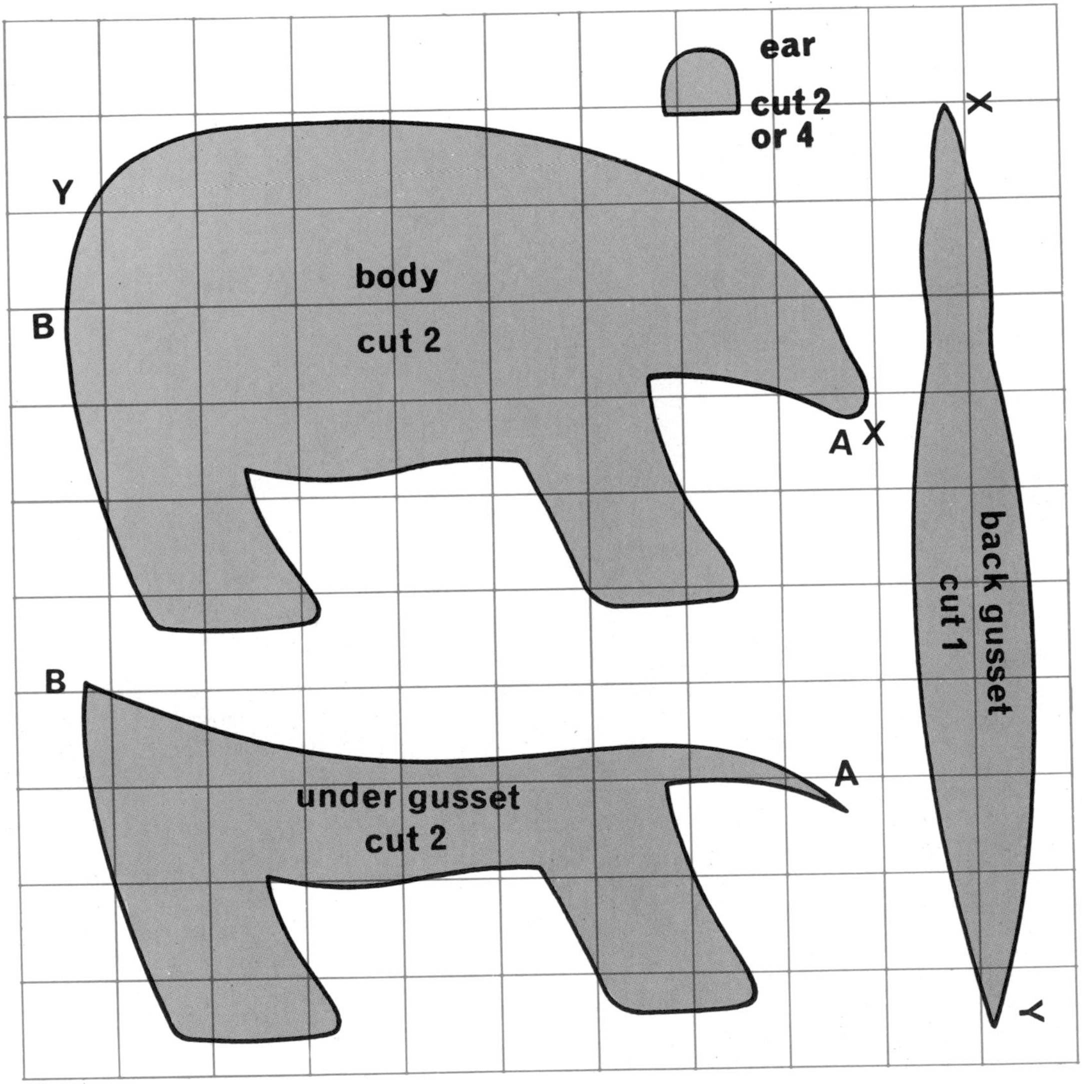

ear
cut 2
or 4

Y

B

body

cut 2

X

A X

back gusset
cut 1

B

under gusset
cut 2

A

X

Y

Fig 43

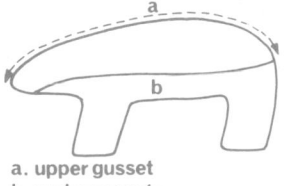

a. upper gusset
b. under gussets

Fig 44

double oversewing

Fig 45

A polar bear and her baby

You will need:

White, fluffy, man-made fibre or white felt which will give a good effect; some kapok or stuffing material; sewing cotton; a strand of black embroidery silk (or black cotton used double would do).

The pattern (Fig 43) is made from a side-view silhouette, the legs rather thick to simulate the thickness of fur. The under gusset is cut from the bottom half of the side shape, from a curving line drawn from under the tail and extended to a tapering point under the chin. The head gusset stretches from the top of the nose, and is shaped for the face, its widest part being over the shoulders (Fig 44).

Make templates in thin card and trace round them on to the wrong side of the man-made fibre, pressing down the edges of the card to keep the material in place, or the outline will waver and be distorted.

Cut two side pieces, two under gussets, two ears, the tail and one top gusset.

All sewing except for the final seam is done on the wrong side. Pin the top gusset to the two side pieces, matching the curves, and sew the seams, using double oversewing, that is, putting the needle twice into the same place (Fig 45). Sew the two under-gusset pieces together and pin to one side piece, matching feet, and sew it into place. Pin the second side in place, but sew only from the chin, round the front leg, and then fasten off. Then sew from the tail round the back leg, leaving the middle seam between the two legs open.

Sew the short seam on the nose between the two gussets.

Turn it inside out and press the seams as flat as possible.

Stuff the head and legs fairly firmly but not too hard or the material will stretch out of shape. Stuff the rest of the body evenly, and sew up the remaining seam with ladder stitch.

Embroider the eyes in circles of straight stitch on the face, just touching the gusset

Fig 46

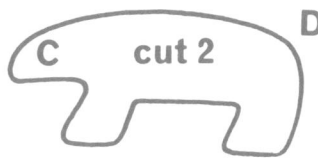

Fig 47

seams, and then embroider the nose. The mouth shape is in single chain stitch as shown (Fig 46). Eyes and nose can be cut from scraps of black felt or Vilene if wished.

Sew four or five straight stitches in black on the front of each foot for claws.

Sew the straight edges of the ears on to the face near the gusset seam with ladder stitch, curving the edges into a horseshoe shape.

A rectangle of man-made fibre folded in half and seamed with one end turned under into a curve forms the tail, sewn on where the two gussets meet.

Her baby has an under gusset to make her stand, but has no top gusset, and needs only a small piece of material (Fig 47). She measures just over 7.5 cm (3″).

Cut two side pieces, one under gusset, one tail and two ears.

Again, sewing is done on the wrong side. Sew the gusset to both side pieces, leaving one middle seam open between the legs. Use double oversewing.

Turn it inside out and finish off like the big bear.

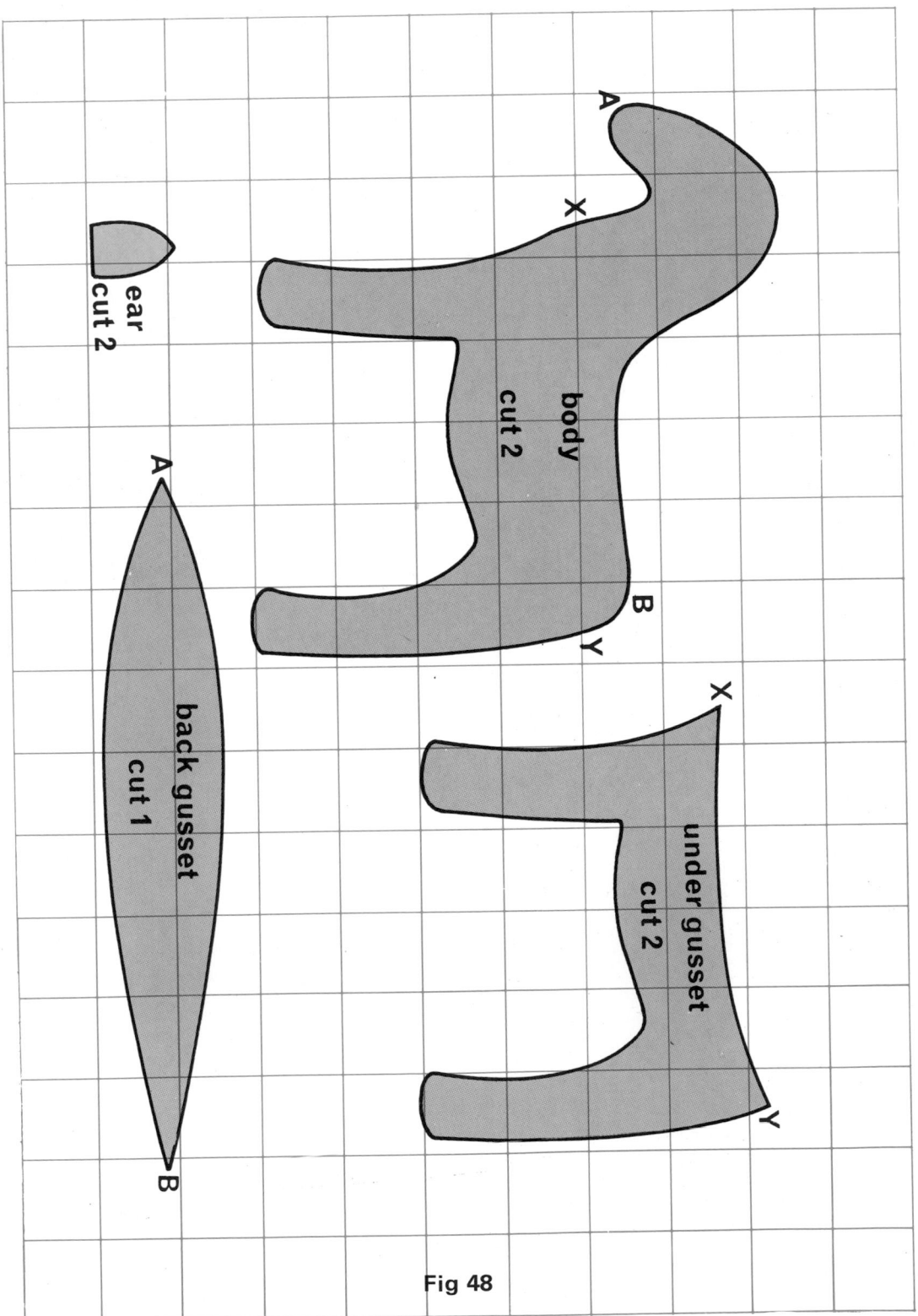

Fig 48

A little standing horse

He is made of pink felt with embroidered legs and trappings and stands just over 15 cm (6"). His mane and tail are of fringed black felt (Fig 48).

You will need:

A piece of felt in the main colour measuring 20 cm by 40 cm (8" by 16"); a small piece of black felt; an oval 5 cm (2") by 7.5 cm (3") for his saddle in a contrasting felt; some embroidery silks, including black; metal-thread; sequins; kapok or similar for stuffing.

He has a long back gusset from nose to tail to give him a round back, and an under gusset to enable him to stand.

If you are making your own template, draw a silhouette with a straight front leg and a hind leg with a slight bend in it. On this side view draw a curved line from the middle of the chest to under the tail, the line following the curve under the body. The ear is a triangle shape with curved sides.

For the top gusset measure from just under the nose, over the head and back, to the tail, and cut the gusset this length, tapering to a point at each end and about 4 cm (1½") wide along the back (Fig 49). The mane is a narrow double strip of black felt long enough to stretch from the forehead over the head down to the base of the neck.

Trace round the template on to the big piece of felt, with a very sharp pencil, reversing the templates for the second sides so that all pencil marks can be kept on the wrong side.

Cut two side pieces, two under gussets, two ears and one top gusset.

Do the embroidery before any sewing up.

For embroidering, draw a simple design on thin paper on to a traced outline of the sides of the horse.

Pin this to the body pieces and sew the design through the paper and felt with small running stitches in contrasting cotton. When the whole design has been sewn, carefully tear away the paper and embroider over the running stitches. If not wholly covered by the embroidery, they can be pulled out. Be careful to work the pieces for right and left sides.

Sew the back gusset to both side pieces,

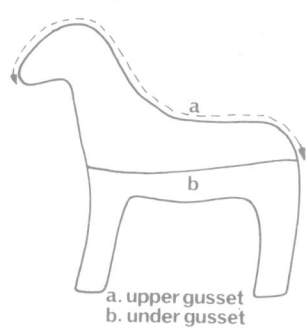

a. upper gusset
b. under gusset

Fig 49

Fig 50

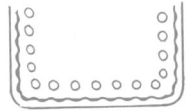

Fig 51

starting each time from the nose and working on the right side. Sew the two under gussets together along the curved seam, on the wrong side, and sew them to one side of the body, matching feet and tops of legs. Sew the seam of the body pieces from the nose to the point of the under gusset.

Stuff the head smoothly, and the two legs already sewn, firmly. Pin the second side of the body to the under gusset and sew round both legs, leaving the seam open between the legs. Stuff the two legs firmly, especially at the top; if there are weak places the horse will not stand up. Stuff the rest of the body evenly with small pieces of stuffing. Sew up the remaining seam.

Embroider an eye (Fig 50) each side in stem stitch, with straight stitches for eye lashes, a single chain stitch for each nostril, and a mouth in stem stitch.

Sew the straight edges of the ears to the head gusset seam, using ladder stitch and curving the corners in to form a horseshoe shape.

Fold the mane in half along its length and snip into a fringe. Sew it down on each side of the fold so that it will stand up on the head and neck. Use ladder stitch to sew it.

Cut a long narrow piece of black felt into a long fringe for a tail and sew it on where the two gussets meet.

Embroider round the edge of the oval of felt for the saddle (Fig 51). This one has an edge of pink running stitches threaded with silver metal-thread and a row of pink sequins sewn inside it. Lay it over the back of the horse and attach it with tiny, invisible stitches. The embroidery on the legs is a wavy line of threaded running stitch in turquoise silk (to match the saddle cloth) and inside one row of blanket stitch in silver metal-thread. Bridle and reins could be added if desired.

A giraffe

He is tall, with long slender legs. He is cut out in natural-coloured felt with chestnut-coloured markings. His colouring has been made with separate, irregular, diamond-shaped pieces sewn on to sides and back.

You will need:

Natural-coloured felt; chestnut-coloured felt; kapok or similar stuffing; beige and chestnut-coloured sewing cotton; black embroidery silk, or double black cotton; light brown wool for tail.

The actual pattern pieces (Fig 53) are not complicated — an upper gusset, shaped over the pointed head, narrowing for the long neck and broadening out over the back to taper to a point at the tail, and the usual under gusset of lower part of body and legs, cut from a curved line from tail to base of neck (Fig 52).

Trace the shapes on to the felt very carefully, especially round the legs, holding the template firmly so that it does not move, and reversing the templates for the second pieces.

Cut two side pieces, two under gussets, two ears and one back gusset from the beige or natural-coloured felt, a number of 1 cm ($\frac{1}{2}$") wide strips, cut into diamond

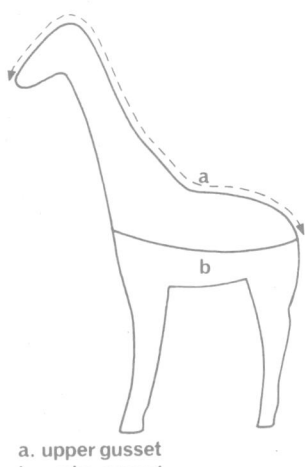

a. upper gusset
b. under gusset

Fig 52

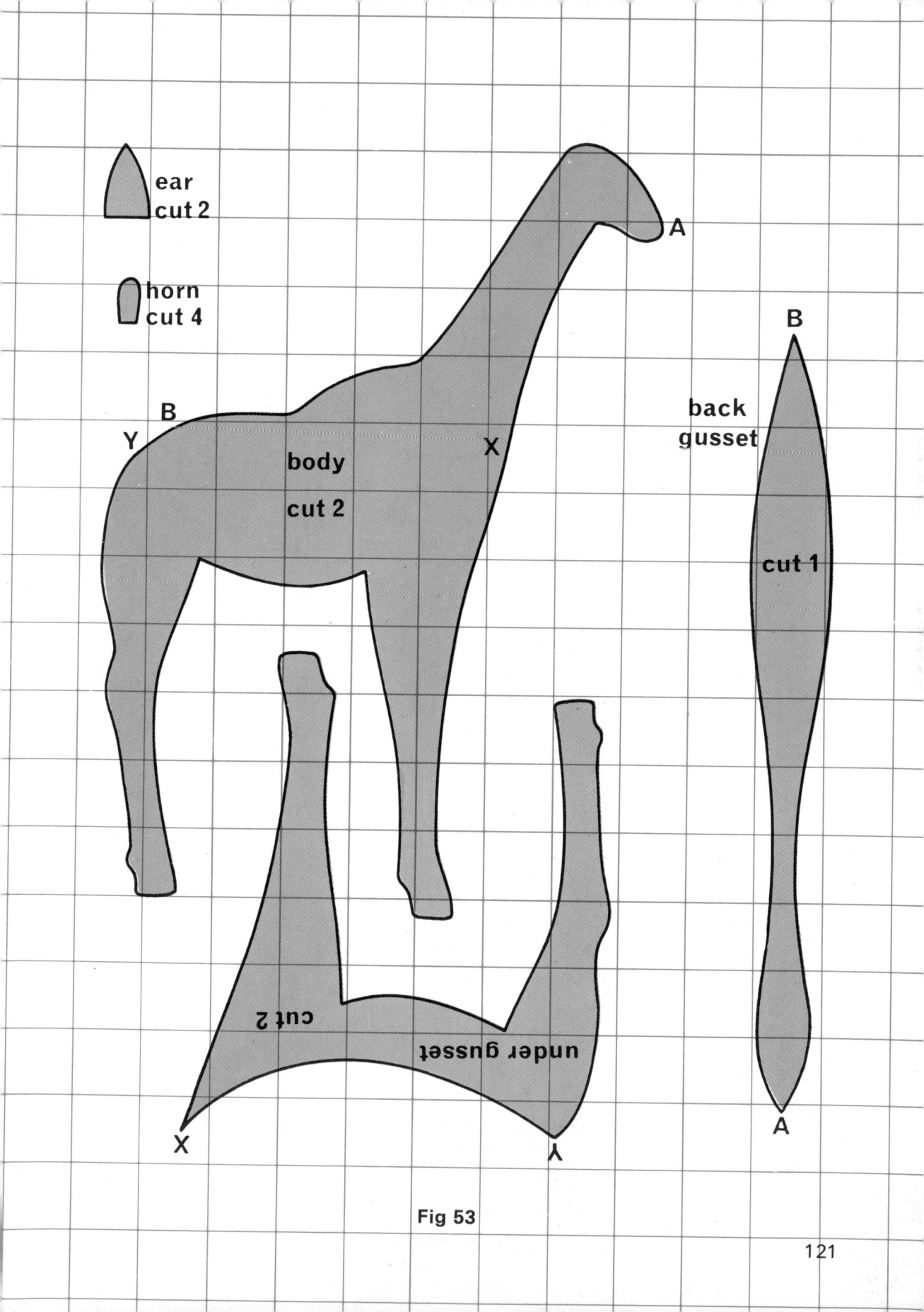

ear
cut 2

horn
cut 4

A

B

body

cut 2

Y

B

X

back
gusset

cut 1

cut 2

under gusset

X

Y

A

Fig 53

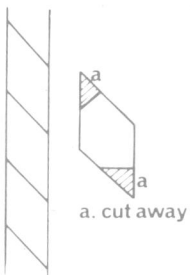

a. cut away

Fig 54

shapes (Fig 54), and four horn shapes from the chestnut felt. Cut the strips of felt. diagonally and trim some of the corners off the pieces to make them irregular in shape.

Sew them in position in three rows, spaced apart, starting with a middle line of them from high on the neck, across the centre of the side and down the back leg. A row of them each side of this, one row across the body and down the front leg, and a second row down the front of the neck and the front of the front leg should be enough. Repeat this on the second side, reversing the side piece so that you have a pair.

Pin the head gusset in place carefully and sew it on to both sides with right sides outside. Stitch some chestnut shapes down the neck and back of the upper gusset, taking one or two over the seams. Join the under gusset pieces along the curved seam, on the wrong side. Pin it to one of the side pieces, matching the feet. Start sewing from the neck down the leg and about 2.5 cm (1") along the inner leg seam.

Because his legs are so slender, they must be stuffed very carefully or the shape will be spoiled. Stuff the leg with *very* small pieces of stuffing, pushing them down into corners and seams with a blunted orange stick, and making it as firm as possible without pulling the stitches. Continue sewing an inch at a time, stuffing as you sew. Continue with the hind leg in the same way. Sew the seam under the chin and about 1 cm ($\frac{1}{2}$") down the neck. Stuff the head. Continue sewing the neck seam, stuffing as you sew.

Make a short cord for the tail by twisting the doubled wool together, sew the ends to keep them in place and fringe them. Push the end under the point at the end of the top gusset and sew in securely.

Pin the second side to the gusset and sew round both legs, stuffing very carefully and very firmly, leaving the seam open between the legs. Stuff the rest of the body, keeping it smooth but not so hard as the legs. Sew up the opening.

Fold the corners of the ears to the centre, and sew them on the sides of the head with ladder stitch so that they stand out at each side. Sew the curved seams of the two little horns, stuff them firmly and sew them on top of the head with ladder stitch, keeping them in an upright position as you sew.

Sew spots in satin stitch for eyes (Fig 55), with straight stitches for the long eye lashes, and two nostrils and a mouth, all in black embroidery silk.

Fig 55

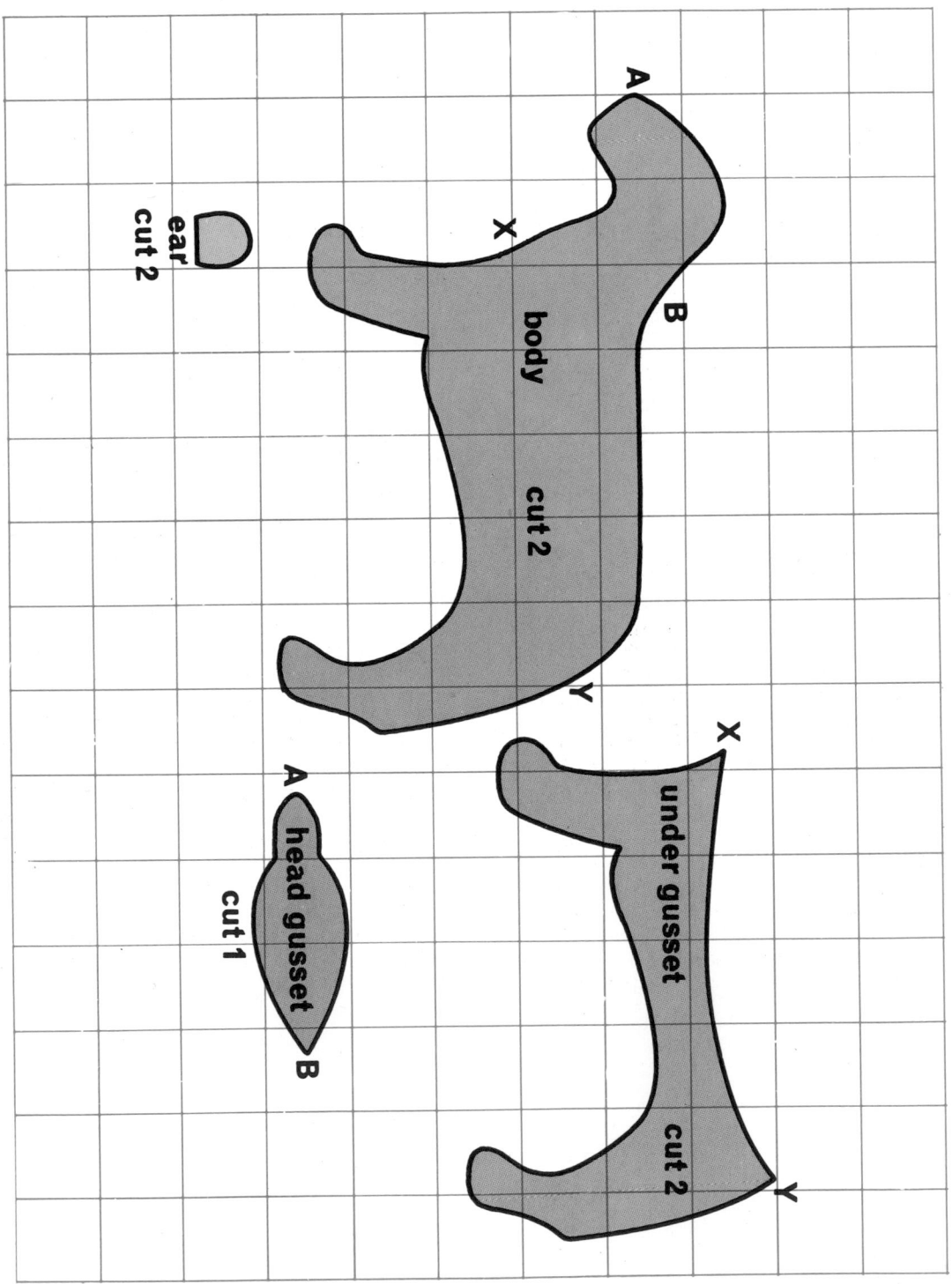

Fig 56

A tiger

You will need:

Orange felt; black and green embroidery silk; kapok for stuffing; orange and white cotton.

The template (Fig 56) is similar to that of the horse. It is made from a silhouette of the tiger, with a small head gusset from the top of the nose to the back of the neck, cut to give a slightly oval shape to the top of the nose, and tapering to a point at the back of the neck. The under gusset consists of the front and back leg, the top being a curving line from the chest to the tail, following the under-body curve.

Make the templates in thin card and trace round them on to the felt, reversing them for the second pieces.

Cut two body pieces, two under gussets, one head gusset and two ears, all in orange felt.

Embroider, using chain stitch, the two side pieces in wavy stripes from the back downwards, in black embroidery silk (Fig 57). Pair them for left and right.

Join the two sides to the head gusset on the right side, starting each time from the nose with the more oval end, and matching the finishing point at the neck.

Embroider more lines on the top and back of the head gusset, extending them over the seams in some cases.

Join the curved sides of the under gusset on the wrong side, and sew one body side piece on to it, starting from the neck. Sew down the front seam of the front leg, along the sole, and about 2.5 cm (1") of the back seam.

Now stuff the foot very firmly with small pieces of kapok. Finish the leg seam and stuff the rest of the leg. Continue along the under body and sew the back leg in a similar manner to the front leg.

Make a cord for a tail with orange cotton, and fringe the end. Pin it in position at the top of the gusset.

Sew the back seam between the two gussets. Sew the seam from the nose to the top of the neck, and stuff the head, pushing stuffing carefully into the seams and keeping the head a good shape.

Pin the under gusset to the second side, matching pinning points at the feet and the tops of the legs.

Sew and stuff the front leg, and then the back leg, leaving the middle of the body seam open for stuffing. Fill the rest of the body, pushing the stuffing well into the tops of the legs to keep them firm. Sew the tail in with the final seam.

The eyes are an open-ended single chain stitch in black embroidery silk with a green spot in the middle. Embroider in black stem-stitch lines each side of the nose, down the nose at the end of the gusset, to within 1 cm ($\frac{3}{8}$") of the bottom, then curl the line round to make the mouth (Fig 58). Embroider white cotton loops for whiskers, cutting the loops to leave about 2 cm ($\frac{3}{4}$") of whisker.

Fold the corners of the ears to the middle and sew them on the side of the head, touching the head gusset at its widest point.

Fig 57

nose embroidery

Fig 58

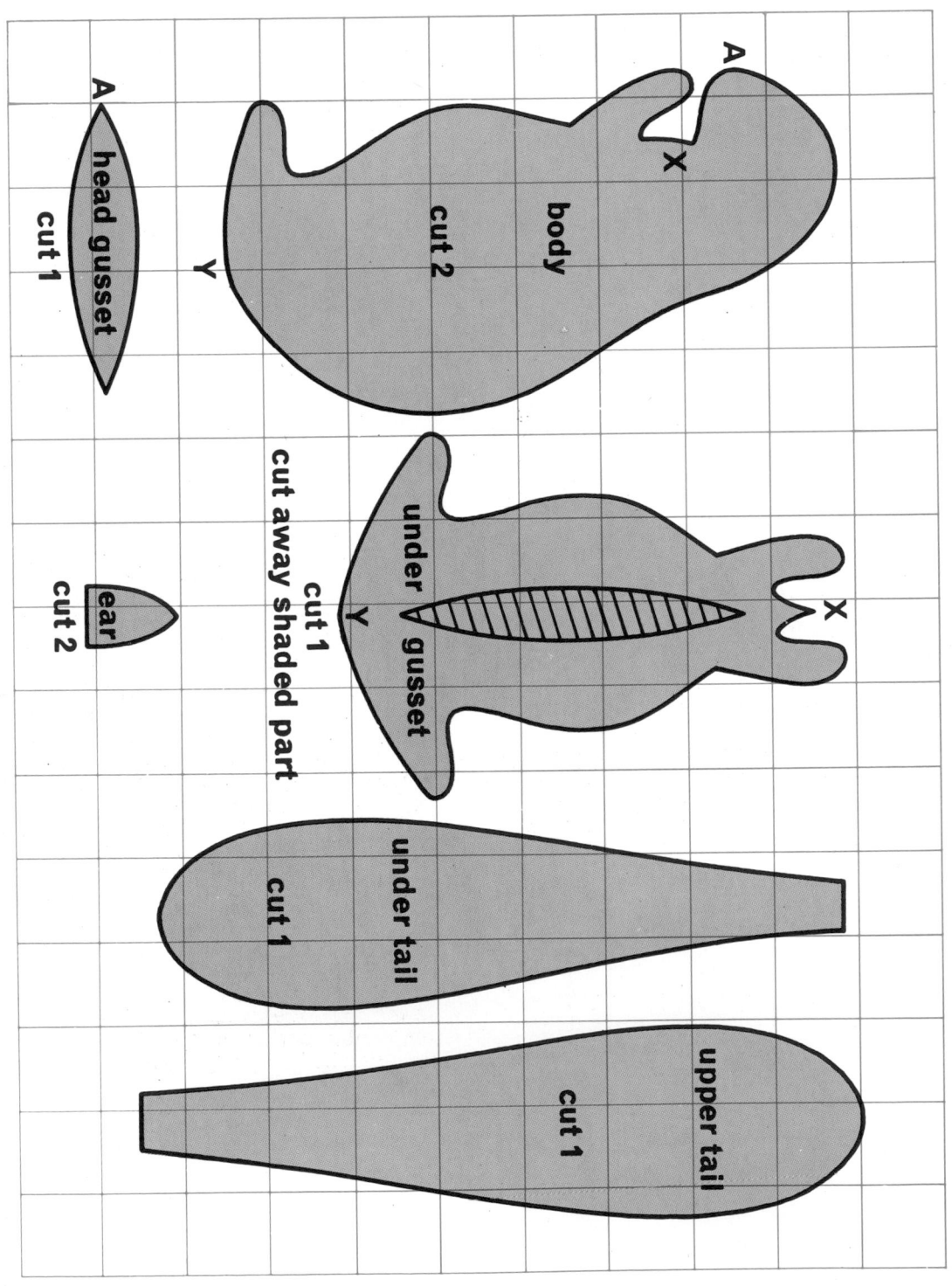

Fig 59

A squirrel

In shape he very much resembles the kangaroo; he is pictured on page 95.

You will need:

Coloured silky wool; dark orange felt for the tail; kapok; a strand of black embroidery silk; matching chestnut-coloured cotton.

The template is again cut from a silhouette drawing, and the under gusset has a curved line following the body line to give a more shaped gusset. The head gusset stretches from the nose to the back of the neck, is pointed at each end and almost 2.5 cm (1") wide on the top of the head. The tail is cut in two parts, the outer piece 6 mm ($\frac{1}{4}$") shorter to make it curl over (Fig 59).

Cut two side pieces, one under gusset, one head gusset and two pointed ears from the chestnut-coloured felt.

Sew the head gusset to the two sides, starting each time from the nose. Cut away the shaded part of the under gusset and sew together on the wrong side the edges thus formed. Sew the back seam, and then sew the under gusset to one of the body pieces at the front. Sew the front seam from the nose, under the chin as far as the gusset.

Stuff the head and the two sewn legs. Sew the second side to the under gusset, stuffing it as you sew.

Embroider two biggish black spots, each surrounded with four straight stitches in a diamond shape, for eyes (Fig 60).

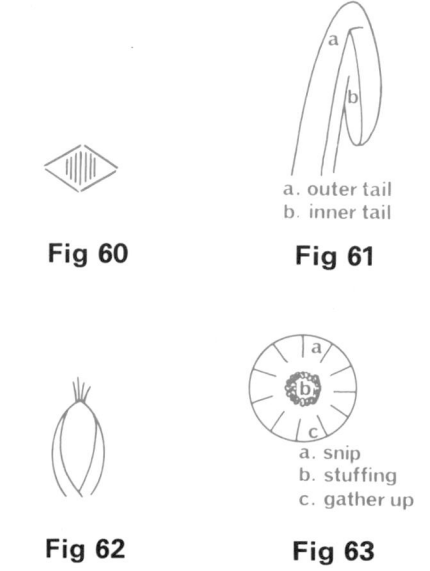

Fig 60   **Fig 61**

a. outer tail
b. inner tail

a. snip
b. stuffing
c. gather up

Fig 62   **Fig 63**

Sew loops of chestnut-coloured cotton for whiskers, and cut and trim them.

Sew together the curved sides of the tail, making a fold across the top so that the wider end curls over (Fig 61). Stuff softly and evenly, keeping it flat. Sew it on at the base of the back so that the end curls outwards, away from the head. With cotton, sew loops of apricot-coloured wool all up the back and over the top of the curled part of the tail. Cut all the loops, and tease out the wool carefully for a fluffy effect.

Unravel a short length of wool and thread a needle with a single ply of it. Sew small tufts on the pointed ends of the ears (Fig 62). Sew the ears on top of the head on the gusset seams, in a horseshoe shape so that they stand upright, with the curve towards the back.

Cut a small oval of orange felt and snip round the edges. Place a ball of stuffing in the centre, gather up the edges and draw up into a ball (Fig 63). Sew it between the paws for a nut.